Quilting, Patchwork and Appliqué

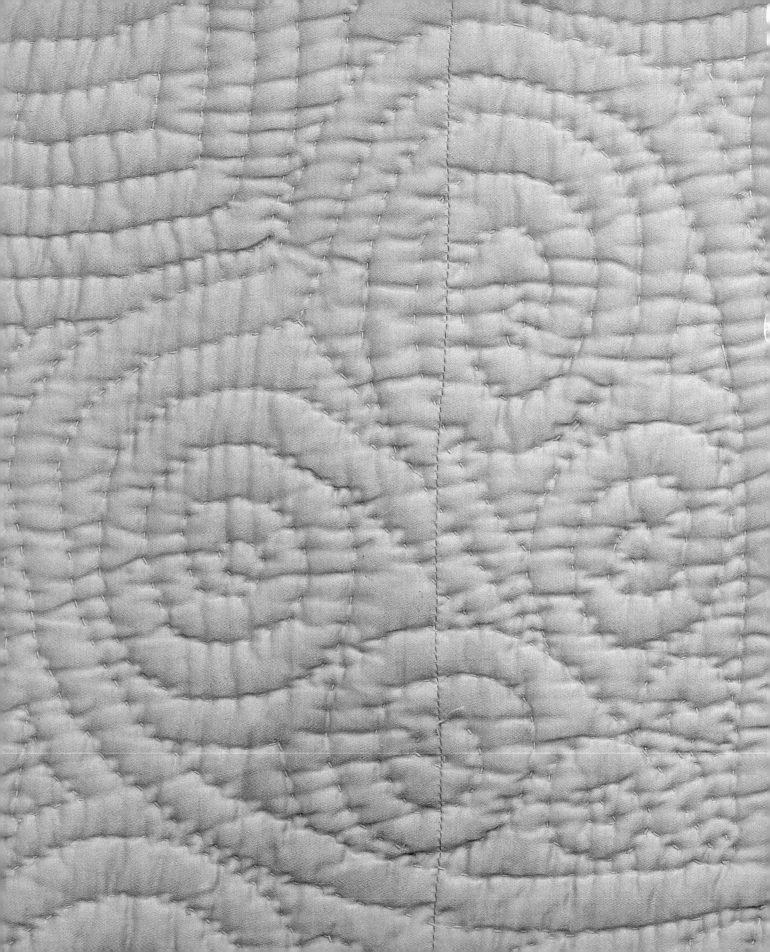

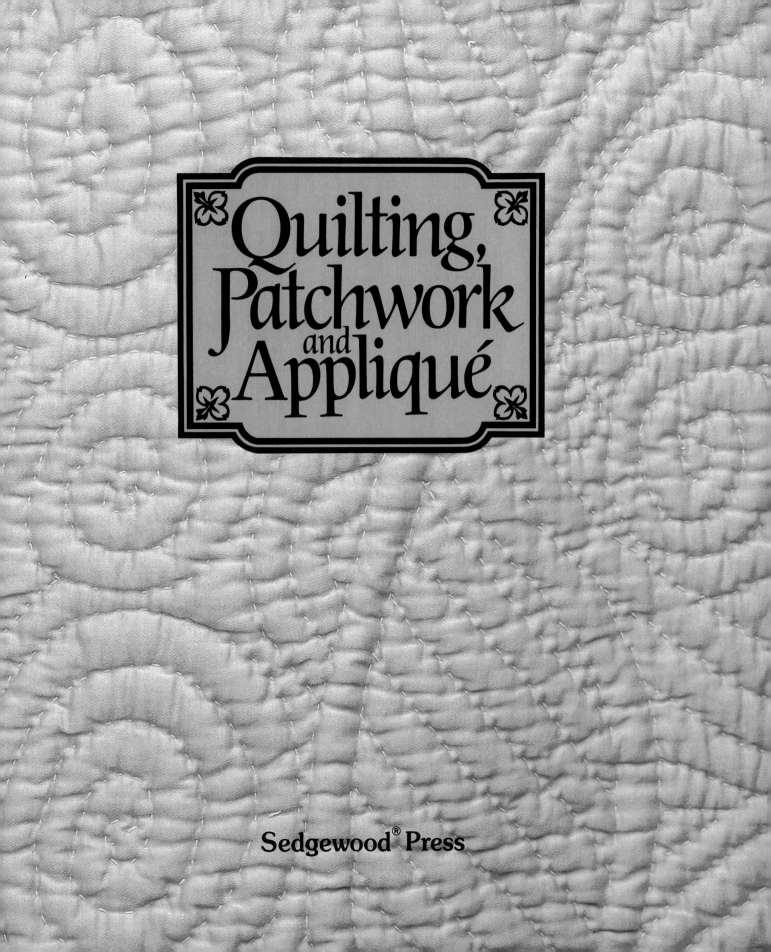

Quilting, Patchwork and Appliqué

Sedgewood® Press

Published by Sedgewood Press

For Sedgewood® Press
Editorial Director: Elizabeth P. Rice
Associate Editor: Leslie Gilbert
Production Manager: Bill Rose

Produced for Sedgewood® Press by
Marshall Cavendish Books Limited
58 Old Compton Street
London W1V 5PA

For Marshall Cavendish
Editor: Eleanor Van Zandt
Designer: Jill Moore
Production Manager: Dennis Hovell

First Printing 1986

© Marshall Cavendish Limited 1986
Distributed by Macmillan Publishing Company,
a division of Macmillan, Inc.

ISBN 0-02-609020-1

Library of Congress Catalog Card
Number 85-51795

Printed in the United States of America

Note: Since this book was edited, it has been discovered that washable fabric-marking pens can eventually damage some fabrics. Their use is therefore not recommended.

Acknowledgments

Fairfield Processing Corporation, for materials on battings

The Patchwork Dog and Calico Cat Ltd, for quilts, cushions and accessories

CONTENTS

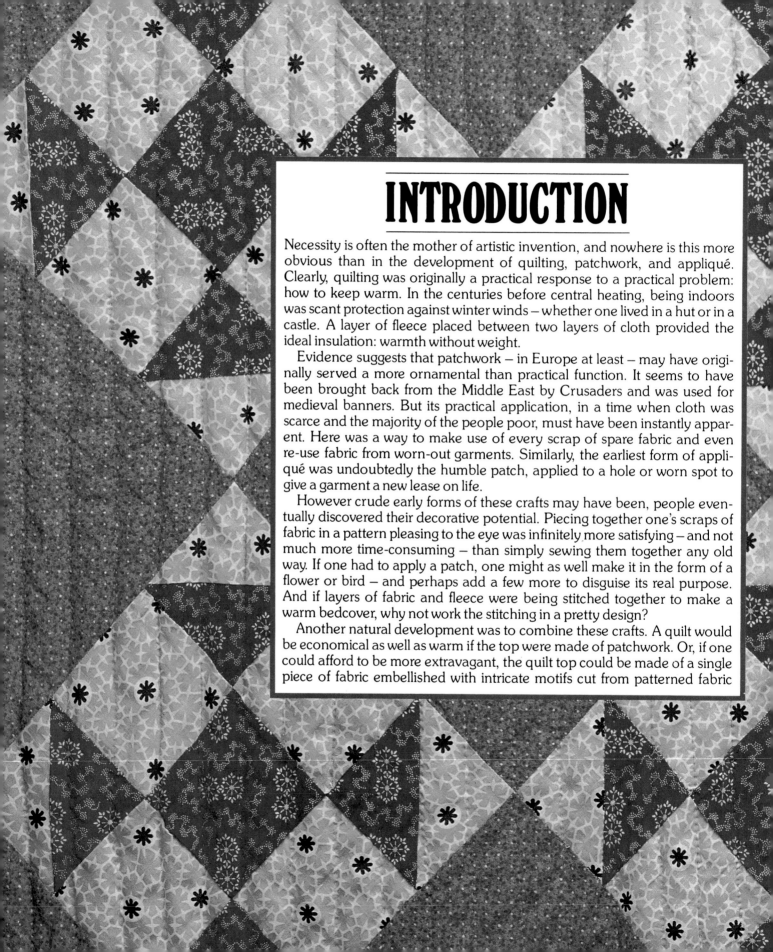

INTRODUCTION

Necessity is often the mother of artistic invention, and nowhere is this more obvious than in the development of quilting, patchwork, and appliqué. Clearly, quilting was originally a practical response to a practical problem: how to keep warm. In the centuries before central heating, being indoors was scant protection against winter winds – whether one lived in a hut or in a castle. A layer of fleece placed between two layers of cloth provided the ideal insulation: warmth without weight.

Evidence suggests that patchwork – in Europe at least – may have originally served a more ornamental than practical function. It seems to have been brought back from the Middle East by Crusaders and was used for medieval banners. But its practical application, in a time when cloth was scarce and the majority of the people poor, must have been instantly apparent. Here was a way to make use of every scrap of spare fabric and even re-use fabric from worn-out garments. Similarly, the earliest form of appliqué was undoubtedly the humble patch, applied to a hole or worn spot to give a garment a new lease on life.

However crude early forms of these crafts may have been, people eventually discovered their decorative potential. Piecing together one's scraps of fabric in a pattern pleasing to the eye was infinitely more satisfying – and not much more time-consuming – than simply sewing them together any old way. If one had to apply a patch, one might as well make it in the form of a flower or bird – and perhaps add a few more to disguise its real purpose. And if layers of fabric and fleece were being stitched together to make a warm bedcover, why not work the stitching in a pretty design?

Another natural development was to combine these crafts. A quilt would be economical as well as warm if the top were made of patchwork. Or, if one could afford to be more extravagant, the quilt top could be made of a single piece of fabric embellished with intricate motifs cut from patterned fabric and sewn on with tiny, invisible stitches. Or one could appliqué small motifs to squares of fabric, join the squares to form a patchwork, and then use the appliqué patchwork as the top of a quilt.

By the early 19th century, these techniques had reached a high degree of refinement and creative invention. In the United States, in particular, the craft of quiltmaking flourished. Hundreds of patchwork patterns were devised, along with innumerable ways of stitching quilt layers together. For the women who painstakingly joined bits of fabric by the light of an oil lamp after the day's work was done and then gathered to work the quilting as a communal activity, the making of a quilt was not just a domestic task but the perpetuating of a tradition and a means of self-expression.

Today, after a period of decline, these three forms of needlework are being revived with enthusiasm and imagination. Traditional patchwork and appliquéd quilts once again adorn beds throughout the country. But in our affluent society people can afford to be more relaxed and more experimental in their approach to needlework. Freed from the necessity of producing a dozen quilts for the household, the modern needleworker can devote her skill and creativity to making other things, just for the fun of it: patchwork placemats, quilted throw pillows, an appliquéd window shade. Old methods from other cultures are adapted; new ones are devised.

The rich diversity of modern quilting, patchwork, and appliqué is well represented in this book. Within its pages you will find traditional designs – both American and British – and modern interpretations of these designs ; simple projects to run up on the machine and elaborate ones to be stitched lovingly and carefully by hand; amusing objects for children and elegant ones for adults; projects that use only one of the techniques and those that incorporate two or even all three. The scope of these enduringly popular needlecrafts is here for you to discover.

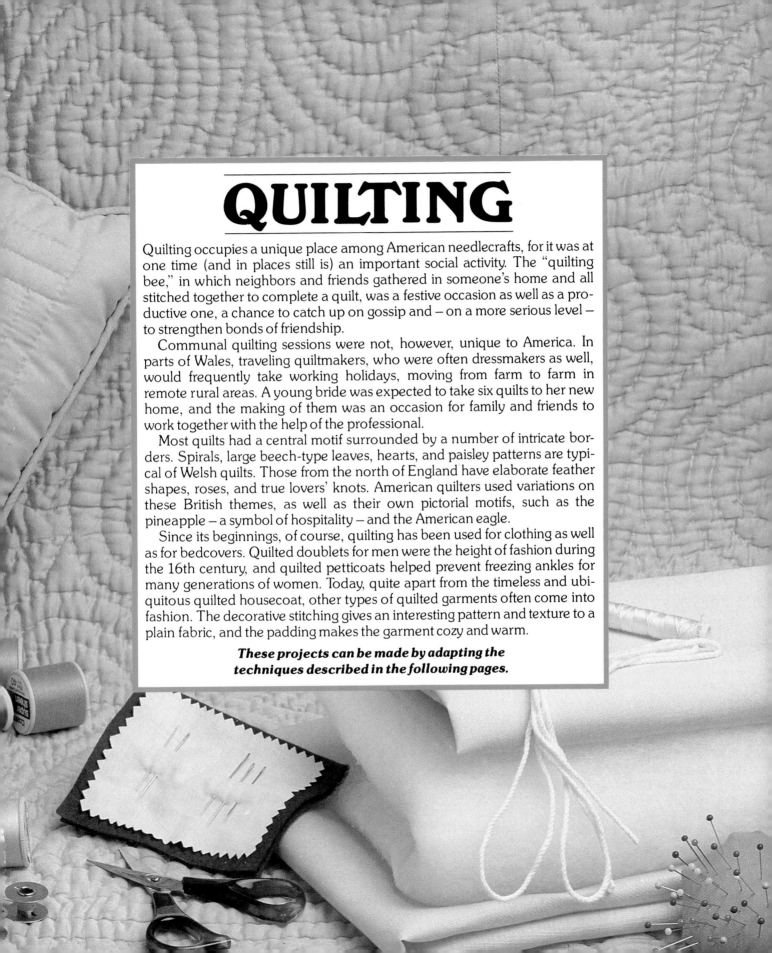

QUILTING

Quilting occupies a unique place among American needlecrafts, for it was at one time (and in places still is) an important social activity. The "quilting bee," in which neighbors and friends gathered in someone's home and all stitched together to complete a quilt, was a festive occasion as well as a productive one, a chance to catch up on gossip and – on a more serious level – to strengthen bonds of friendship.

Communal quilting sessions were not, however, unique to America. In parts of Wales, traveling quiltmakers, who were often dressmakers as well, would frequently take working holidays, moving from farm to farm in remote rural areas. A young bride was expected to take six quilts to her new home, and the making of them was an occasion for family and friends to work together with the help of the professional.

Most quilts had a central motif surrounded by a number of intricate borders. Spirals, large beech-type leaves, hearts, and paisley patterns are typical of Welsh quilts. Those from the north of England have elaborate feather shapes, roses, and true lovers' knots. American quilters used variations on these British themes, as well as their own pictorial motifs, such as the pineapple – a symbol of hospitality – and the American eagle.

Since its beginnings, of course, quilting has been used for clothing as well as for bedcovers. Quilted doublets for men were the height of fashion during the 16th century, and quilted petticoats helped prevent freezing ankles for many generations of women. Today, quite apart from the timeless and ubiquitous quilted housecoat, other types of quilted garments often come into fashion. The decorative stitching gives an interesting pattern and texture to a plain fabric, and the padding makes the garment cozy and warm.

These projects can be made by adapting the techniques described in the following pages.

QUILTING BASICS

Apart from purely decorative types, such as Italian quilting, all quilting consists essentially of a "sandwich" of two (sometimes more) layers of fabric enclosing a soft filling material and held together by stitching.

The simplest kind of quilting is tied, or tufted, quilting, in which one or more strands of thread are taken through the fabric twice and then tied in a knot, the knots being spaced at regular intervals over the fabric. The crib quilt on page 27 is an example of this kind of quilting.

More often, the layers are held together with lines of stitching. The lines may echo those of a patchwork design or appliqué motif, or they may form a design of their own. They may be worked by hand or by machine.

Designing

Suitable designs for quilting are easy to find. Many needlework shops offer a selection of stencils designed specifically for quilting, and some of these can be specially ordered in a size to suit a particular project. For a repeating design you can make a cardboard template (such as the clamshell shown on page 120) and draw around it on the fabric. Overlapping circles produced in this way make an attractive quilting design. Another approach is to draw a design on paper and transfer it to the fabric using the pricking method shown on page 12. The design might be traced from a piece of printed fabric or wallpaper, or adapted from a painting or photograph.

Materials

When planning a quilting design, it is important to consider the relationship between the design, the fabric, and the filler, or batting. If the design is complex, it is best worked on a solid-colored fabric (preferably in a light color), which will show the stitching and the shadows it produces more clearly. Small prints can work well, but larger ones are best avoided.

It is also best to choose a fairly thin batting, which will facilitate working the tiny stitches required for an intricate design. In any case, concentrated areas of stitching will flatten the batting, making unstitched areas of thick batting look odd. If a puffy effect is desired, keep the design simple.

In the past, batting was made of cotton or wool. Today, cotton and even sometimes wool battings are still available, although the cotton often contains a small percentage of polyester. Some quilters prefer such traditional battings for their flattish texture. However, cotton batting does have a tendency to shift unless the quilting covers the surface fairly densely, and it should not be washed. Far more widely used these days is polyester batting, which comes in various thicknesses and is washable. It is much springier than cotton. Batting comes in a wide range of widths, up to 120 in, which will make a quilt for a king-size bed. If, however, you need to join widths of batting to make a piece of the required size, you should cut and join it as shown at left, to avoid producing a ridge that would spoil the finished work.

The bottom layer of the "sandwich," usually called the backing, can be a soft fabric, such as lawn or muslin, if the quilting is to be made into a pillow cover or have a separate lining. If you are making a quilt, however, you should use fabric similar to the top fabric in weight and quality.

Method of joining batting

HAND QUILTING

The techniques involved in hand quilting are essentially simple ones, but they require a degree of patience. For the work to be attractive, all the stitches must be the same length. This is more important than their being tiny, although the smaller they are, the better. Before quilting can begin, careful basting is necessary to ensure that the layers are absolutely smooth.

Some people prefer to quilt with the work mounted in a frame or quilting hoop, others prefer to spread the work on a table or, if it is small, to hold it in the lap. Large quilting frames of the type used at the traditional quilting bee take up an enormous amount of room, but a modern adaptation, which can be adjusted to different widths and tilts for ease of working, is a good investment if you plan to do a lot of quilting.

Quilting hoops are basically large embroidery hoops, often oval in shape. Those that stand on the floor are easiest to use, because they leave both hands free (see step 7, page 14). Their only disadvantages are that the work must be moved occasionally and that additional strips of fabric must be sewn to the sides for holding the corners in the hoop.

A large project, such as a quilt, can be placed on a table with half of the work rolled up and held in place with weights and the other half hanging off the front edge and partly supported in the lap.

Whichever method you choose, you will find it easiest to stitch toward yourself, turning the work or shifting your position as the design dictates. It is a good idea to keep several needles in the work at a time so that several lines can be worked in one direction before turning.

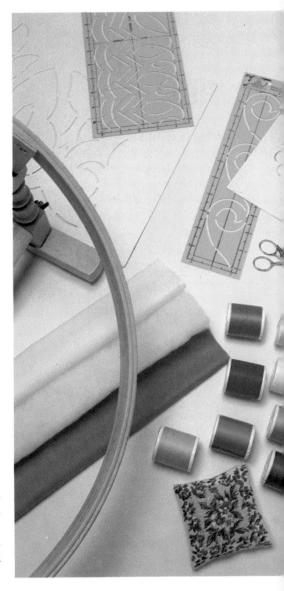

Fabrics Soft fabrics woven from natural fibers are best for hand quilting, since they are easy to sew. Because the line produced by running stitches is a broken line, a patterned fabric will tend to obscure it; choose a solid color and a smooth texture for the best results. Make sure that the top fabric and the backing are pre-shrunk and, if two or more colors are used, that they are colorfast.

Threads Use a thread a shade or two darker than the fabric to accentuate the design. Quilting thread, which may be all cotton or cotton-wrapped polyester, is a strong, lustrous thread treated to resist knotting. It comes in a wide selection of colors. You can, if you like, use ordinary polyester-cotton sewing thread, but you should first run it through a cake of beeswax to prevent tangles. Silk twist can be used for a richer effect. Certain embroidery threads, such as pearl cotton and coton à broder, lend themselves well to hand quilting.

Sewing equipment A betweens needle, size 8 or 9, is best-suited to hand quilting because it is short and maneuverable. A crewel needle, which has a large eye, must be used with thicker threads. Fine silk pins should be used when pinning layers together, as they will not leave marks on the fabric.

A thimble is essential for quilting. If you are using a hoop or frame, you should also wear a special quilter's thimble, which has a flat top, on the hand underneath the work.

You will also need a sharp pair of dressmaker's scissors for cutting fabric and embroidery scissors for snipping threads.

Materials for transferring designs For marking the lines of a stencil or the edges of a template, you have a choice of materials. A silver-colored pencil, available in quilters' shops, makes a fine line, visible on most fabrics. It is easily covered by the stitches, but is indelible. Or you can use a dressmaker's marking pen, which is washable (test it first on your fabric) and produces a thicker line. A white soapstone marker is a good choice for a medium- to dark-toned fabric. Its thin line can be rubbed out if you make a mistake.

If you are using the pricking method of transferring a design (see below), you will also need some powder for rubbing through the holes (a special powder called "pounce" is made for this purpose, although talcum powder will do) and a small piece of felt.

Ready-made stencils can be purchased from quilters' shops, but if you want to make your own you will need some stiff paper or cardboard, a craft knife for cutting the lines (which should be about ⅛ in wide), and a thick piece of cardboard to protect the working surface. To make a template, you will also need thick cardboard, as well as a sharp pencil and – depending on the shape – a right-angled triangle and a compass.

Pricking transfer method

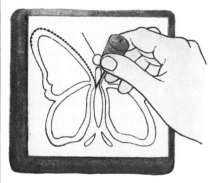 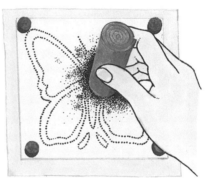 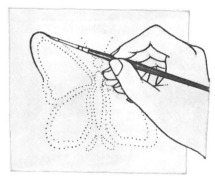

1 Trace the design and place it on a padded surface (upside down if it is asymmetrical). Set the eye of a sewing needle into a cork and prick along the lines of the design. On fine double lines, such as flower stems, prick only one line, to ensure that the markings are covered completely by the embroidery.

2 Place the paper, rough side up, over the fabric and weight each corner. Using a roll of felt, rub pounce (a mixture of chalk and charcoal) or talcum powder carefully over the surface so that it goes through the holes.

3 Remove the paper carefully, leaving trails of small dots. Join up the dots using a pencil or very fine paintbrush and either oil or poster paint. Test the paint on the edge of the fabric to make sure it is not too wet. (Never use ball point or felt-tip pen.)

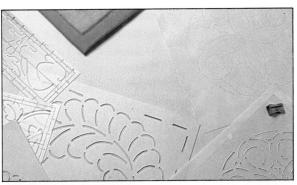

1 Cutting and marking the fabric It is important to cut the three layers slightly larger than the required size. This allows for final trimming and also for the natural shrinkage due to quilting. It is easier to mark the design first on the top fabric before the layers are assembled.. Trace around the stencil lightly, using a fabric-marking pencil.

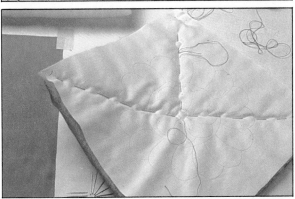

2 Basting the layers together Lay the backing fabric wrong side up on a flat surface (the corners can be secured with masking tape). Place the batting and the top fabric on top. Pin the layers together in the center, at the edges, and elsewhere, as necessary. Baste them together, starting at the center and leaving a long tail, then working toward one corner. Fasten off, then baste to the opposite corner, using the tail of thread. This eliminates knots at the center, which might obscure the design.

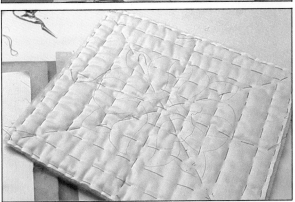

3 Completing the basting After basting a diagonal cross, baste as before, vertically and horizontally. Then work concentric lines of basting, as shown. This method helps to keep the fabric smooth and prevents excess fabric from accumulating at the center.

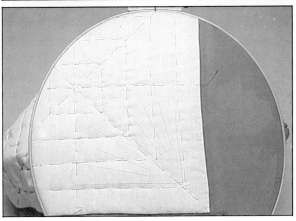

4 Mounting the work in a hoop If you are using a quilting hoop, you will need to baste strips of fabric (such as firmly-woven heavy cotton) to the edges of the work, so that the corners can be worked in the hoop. Cut the strips about 5 in or 6 in wide. When beginning to quilt, center the work on the hoop. Place it over the inner ring, then press the outer ring down over it. If necessary, the screw can be tightened to hold the work more securely.

5 Beginning to quilt Thread the needle with about 18 in of thread, knotted at the end. Bring the thread up through the backing at the center of the design. Give the thread a little tug to bring the knot up into the batting; the end can simply be trimmed. Work with a small, evenly-spaced running stitch. Evenness is more important than the size of the stitches.

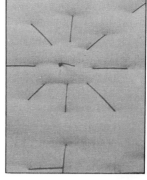 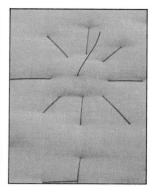

6 To quilt in the hand, use a thimble on the middle finger of the stitching hand, as shown, and work toward yourself. Place the other hand under the work to check that the needle goes through all layers. Keep the thumb pressed down on the fabric just ahead of the quilting line. With practice it is possible to take several stitches at a time and build up a steady rhythm.

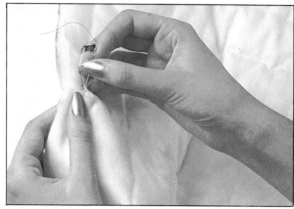

7 To quilt in a hoop or frame Keep the non-stitching hand under the work. On the index finger of this hand wear a quilter's thimble (or an ordinary thimble flattened at the top by a hammer). Push this finger up against the backing to form a ridge on the work. Push the needle into this ridge and back up to the top. Press the thumb of the sewing hand on the fabric just ahead of the quilting line, and take one stitch at a time.

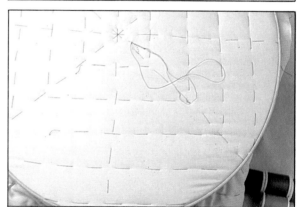

8 Finishing off To finish off, tie a knot close to the last stitch on the top of the work. Take the thread into the batting for a short distance, hiding the knot, then bring it to the top and cut the thread. Another method is to make a small backstitch through the top and batting only, pierce the stitch with the needle to anchor it, then take the thread through the batting and back up to the top and cut.

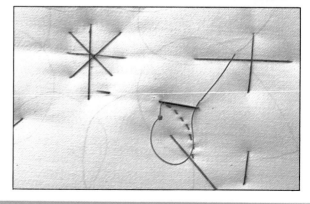

QUILTING PATTERNS

1 Cable designs
These two cable designs are easy to work and make attractive borders. The sample is worked in silk thread on shot silk fabric.

1

2

2 Quilted letters
Outline the letters and place them in relief by quilting the background closely. The sample is worked in buttonhole twist on cotton satin.

3

3 Embroidered corners
A variety of embroidery stitches can be used to quilt small motifs like these. The ones used here are: chain, twisted chain, herringbone, chevron, threaded running, and backstitch. Glossy embroidery threads contrast effectively with textured cotton.

4 Complex cable
Worked singly or in pairs, this design makes an interesting border. (The sample is worked in crochet cotton on glazed polyester cotton.) It can also be used effectively as a repeating design, as shown in this tied pillow cover.

4

5 Byzantine knot
This attractive motif is worked in quilting thread on cotton satin. It can be used singly or as a repeat pattern.

6 Art Nouveau corner
Use this stylish corner to finish a simple line border or as a motif in its own right. The sample is worked in silk thread on glazed polyester cotton, using a lightweight batting.

7 Peony
Outline the flower in running stitch and give contours to the center with seeding and bullion knots. The sample is worked in silk thread on silk fabric over a cotton batting.

HAND-QUILTED PILLOWS

Creamy, lustrous cotton is used for these elegant throw pillows. If you prefer, you could make them in a pale pastel to match your décor. Use the quilting patterns provided or a stencil of your own choice for the design.

Size
18 in square

You will need:
(for one pillow)

1⅜ yd of 36 in-wide dressweight cotton

Piece of lawn or muslin for backing, 24 in square

Piece of lightweight polyester batting, 24 in square

2¼ yd of narrow filler cord

16 in zipper (optional)

Pillow form 18 in square

Quilting thread to match fabric

Quilting hoop (optional)

Betweens needle, size 8 or 9

Tracing paper

Thin cardboard

Large piece of cardboard to work on

Fabric-marking pen

Masking tape

Sewing equipment and threads

Working the quilting

1 Trace the chosen patterns given below (enlarging them if necessary), and tape the tracings to a piece of cardboard. Cut out the templates.

2 From the cotton fabric cut a piece 24 in square. Fold it in quarters, pressing each fold.

3 Fasten the fabric to the working surface with masking tape. Using the fabric-marking pen, carefully draw around the templates.

4 Assemble the three layers – backing, batting, and top fabric – and pin them together at the center and the corners. Then baste them together as shown in steps 2 and 3, page 13.

5 Mount the work in the quilting hoop – if you are using one – so that it is centered. (Depending on the size of the hoop and on the design you are working, you may need to baste strips of fabric to the edges of the work.)

6 Using a single strand of quilting thread in the needle, work running stitch along the design lines. Work from the center of the design outward.

Assembling the cover

1 Remove the basting. Trim the work to measure 19 in square, and baste around the edges to hold the layers together.

2 Cut another piece of the fabric, 19 in square. If you are cording the edges, cut enough 2 in-wide bias strips (see page 166) to cover the filler cord. Join the strips and cover the cord.

3 Pin and baste the cord around the edges of the quilted top, placing the stitching line of the cord ½ in from the edge so that the cord lies toward the center. Baste it in place, joining the ends of the cord as shown on page 166.

4 Place the back of the cover on the top piece with right sides facing. Pin and baste them together, then stitch (using the zipper foot if the edges are corded), leaving an opening about 10 in long in one side. If a zipper is to be inserted, leave 16½ in open, but stitch the cording to the top.

5 Press the stitching. Grade the seam, and turn the cover right side out.

6 Insert the zipper, if desired, basting each tape to the opening edges, then hand-sewing it, using a small, spaced backstitch. On the corded side, hide the stitches in the seam joining the cording. Insert the pillow form.

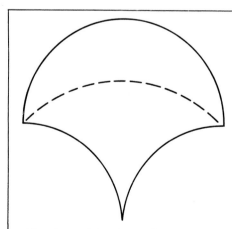

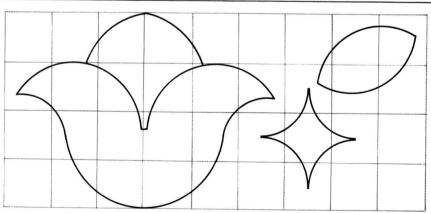

Use shape A for the scallop-design pillow, placing it diagonally and butting the edges as shown in the

photograph. Make a separate template, cutting along the broken line, for the inner curve. Use shapes

B, C, and D for the floral design pillow, enlarging them and positioning them as in the photograph.

HAND QUILTING

TUDOR ROSE PLACEMATS

These bright red placemats, quilted in a traditional English motif, give a festive look to the table. A harmonizing printed fabric is used for lining and binding the edges and, if you like, for matching napkins.

Working the quilting

1 Trace the rose design given below. Cut it out and glue it to a piece of thin cardboard, then cut out the cardboard template.

2 For the leaf design, take a piece of tracing paper at least 12 in square and trace the stem only (leaving room for the leaves) along the lower and right-hand edges of the paper. Also mark the top edge of the shading. Turn the paper over, positioning the shading edge mark correctly, and trace the line again, back to the left-hand edge. Reverse the paper twice more to complete the remaining portions of the stem. Trace the leaves onto the stem. You can trace them so that they point counter-clockwise all the way around, as on the mat shown, or you can reverse their direction at top and bottom.

3 Cut a piece of the top fabric 13½ in square. Fold it horizontally, then vertically, in half, pressing each fold. Baste along each line to mark the center, then press again to remove the creases.

4 Lay the fabric, right side up, on a flat surface and hold it in place with bits of masking tape. Place the rose template in the center, aligning the broken lines with the basting, and draw around it with the fabric marking pencil.

5 Measure 3 in out along each line of basting and make a small mark. Using a right-angled triangle (with the two perpendicular edges placed on marks) and the marking pencil, join up these marks to form a 6 in square. Similarly,

draw a 10 in square around it.

6 Position the leaf tracing on the fabric, centering it carefully. Slip dressmaker's carbon under the tracing. Weight the tracing to keep it in place and go over the lines firmly with ball-point pen or a hard pencil to transfer them to the fabric.

7 Mark 3 more lines around the edge of the fabric, parallel to the sides of the 10 in square and ⅜ in apart.

8 Mark the diagonal lines in the center square, using a ruler as a guide and placing the lines about ½ in apart.

9 Cut a 13½ in square of the lining fabric. Place it wrong side up on a flat surface and lay the batting and top fabric on top of it. Pin, then baste from the center outward and in parallel lines as shown in steps 2 and 3, page 13. (If you are using a quilting or embroidery hoop, you will need to baste extra strips of fabric to the edges, as shown in step 4, page 13.) Mount the work in a hoop, if you are using one.

10 Using quilting thread and the betweens needle, quilt along the design lines, working from the center outward and making small, even running stitches. Take care to conceal the thread ends (see steps 5 and 8, page 14), as the lining should look as neat as the right side.

Napkin

If you want a matching napkin, cut a 13½ in square from the printed fabric. Hem or fringe the edges of the printed square. To fringe, first stitch with a narrow zigzag ½ in from each edge, then unravel the outer threads. To hem, turn under a ¼ in-wide double hem and stitch by machine close to the edge.

Binding

1 From the remaining printed fabric, cut and join enough 1¼ in-wide strips to make a strip 54 in long (see page 166). Turn under and press ¼ in on both long edges.

2 Unfold one edge and place it right side down on the top of the placemat, with the crease ¼ in from the edge. Pin and baste the binding around all four edges, mitering the corners as shown on page 167. Trim the overlapping end and turn under ¼ in for a neat finish. Stitch the binding in place directly on the crease.

3 Turn the binding to the underside. Fold under ¼ in on the raw edge, and baste it in place, mitering the corners. Slipstitch it over the line of machine stitching.

Size
13½ in square

You will need;
(for one placemat and matching napkin)

⅞ yd of 36 in-wide dressweight cotton in a solid color

⅞ yd of 36 in-wide dressweight cotton in a harmonizing print

Piece of lightweight polyester batting 13½ in square

Quilting thread

Betweens needle, size 8

Quilting or embroidery hoop (optional)

Tracing paper

Small piece of thin cardboard

Ruler

Right-angled triangle

Dressmaker's carbon paper

Fabric-marking pencil

Masking tape

Sewing equipment and threads

WRAPPED AND TIED PILLOW COVER

Size
approximately 12 in square when assembled

You will need:

½ yd of 36 in-wide soft cotton or cotton-polyester fabric in a solid color for the quilted cover

¼ yd of 36 in-wide fabric in a contrasting color for binding

Piece of lightweight polyester batting, 16½ in square

½ yd of 36 in-wide fabric for the inner pillow cover

1 skein each of 2 shades of coton à broder to match and harmonize with the binding fabric

Crewel needle, size 5 or 6

Pillow form, 13 in square

Quilting or embroidery frame (optional)

Tracing paper

Dressmaker's carbon paper

Ruler

Right-angled triangle

Sewing equipment and threads

Hand quilting in contrasting embroidery threads forms the design on this novel pillow cover, which has the practical advantage of being easily removed for laundering.

The quilted cover

1 On a large sheet of tracing paper draw the complete design for the quilting as shown opposite. First mark off an area 16 in square, using the triangle to ensure square corners. Join the mid-points of each side of the square and draw another square diagonally inside the first. Mark off the basic grid pattern of 2 in squares. Then fill in the corners with the small quilting patterns tracing them from the full-size squares.

2 Cut 2 pieces of the main fabric, each 16½ in square. Fix one piece to a flat surface with bits of masking tape, and center the tracing on top. Slide the dressmaker's carbon between the tracing and the fabric, and go over all the lines firmly with a ball-point pen or hard pencil.
3 Place the other fabric square wrong side up on a flat surface, and lay the batting and top fabric on top. Pin and baste them together as shown in steps 2 and 3, page 13. Mount the work in the hoop, if you are using one.
4 Using a single strand of coton à broder in the crewel needle and starting at the center of the design, work running stitch along the quilting lines. Use the lighter-colored thread for the central diagonal square and the grid lines within it and both the dark and light thread for the smaller motifs (see photo).
5 Cut 4 strips of binding fabric, each 1½ in wide: 2 strips 16½ in long and 2 strips 36 in long. Turn under and press ¼ in on each long edge of each strip.
6 Unfold one edge of a short strip and place it on one side of the quilted piece, with the right side of the strip to the top of the quilting and raw edges even. Pin, baste (optional), and stitch along the crease. Turn the strip to the underside and baste the folded edge over the stitching. Slipstitch the edge in place. Join the other short strip to the opposite edge in the same way.
7 Attach the longer strips to the remaining sides, as described in step 6, centering them so that the ties are even. Turn in the raw edges at each end, and slipstitch the folded edges together.

The inner pillow
1 Cut 2 squares of the contrasting fabric, each measuring 13 in. Pin them together with right sides facing, and stitch ½ in from the edge, leaving a gap of 10 in in one side. Trim the seam and turn the cover right side out.
2 Insert the pillow form. Slipstitch the opening edges together.
3 Tie the cover around the pillow as shown.

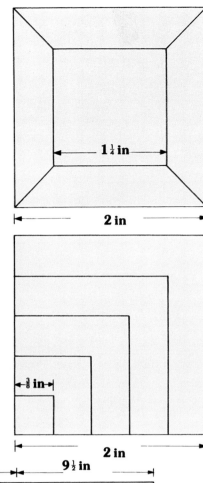

Quilting patterns, actual size, for cover (above) and diagram of complete cover (left)

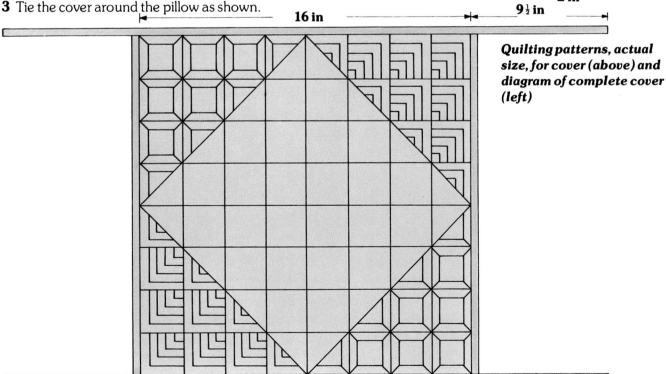

HEART MOTIF CRIB QUILT

Rows of hearts, each quilted in a different pattern, form the design on this charming little quilt. The stitches are worked in shades of blue and violet embroidery thread to match the binding.

Working the quilting

1 Begin by making the template. Using graph paper ruled in $\frac{1}{4}$ in squares, mark off an area 6$\frac{1}{2}$ in square. Darken the first and second lines in from each edge of the square, leaving an area 5$\frac{1}{2}$ in square, then divide the whole square into 8 equal sections as shown in step 1, below.

2 Trace the heart shape given on page 26, using a soft pencil. Place this, wrong side down, on the graph paper, centering it carefully, then go over the line with a ball point pen or hard pencil to transfer the original traced line to the graph paper. Join the center points of the square to form a diamond shape, as shown in step 2, below.

3 Cut a strip of the graph paper 2 in by 9 in, following the lines of the grid. Darken the line in the center (see step 3, below). Place the strip along one side of the diamond and mark points $\frac{1}{4}$ in apart along its length. Repeat on the remaining three sides. Join the dots to make a diagonal grid, using a pencil contrasting in color with the original grid lines. These lines will serve as a guide when marking quilting patterns.

4 Glue the graph pattern to a piece of thin cardboard. Using a sharp craft knife, cut out the heart shape, then cut along the outer lines of the square.

5 Cut the main fabric in half crosswise. Set one piece aside for the back of the quilt. Fold the other piece horizontally and vertically into quarters, pressing each fold. Baste along the fold lines, and press again to remove the creases. Stick the fabric to a flat surface with pieces of masking tape.

6 Place the template on the fabric so that the center horizontal line and one vertical edge are aligned with the basting lines. Using the fabric marking pencil or pen, lightly draw around the heart shape. Mark the outer edges of the template with dots.

7 To draw the quilting lines, first secure the template with masking tape. Then, using a ruler and the horizontal, vertical, or diagonal lines as guides, mark the desired quilting pattern within the heart shape.

8 Move the template to one side of the first marked square, aligning its edge with the dots, and mark another motif, using a different quilting pattern.

Size
approximately 27 in by 34 in

You will need:

2 yd of 36 in-wide cream-colored cotton-wool blend fabric

$\frac{3}{8}$ yd of 36 in-wide printed cotton-wool blend fabric

Piece of lightweight polyester batting, 36 in square

1 skein of coton à broder in each of 8 to 10 colors, to harmonize with printed fabric

Crewel needle, size 5 or 6

Graph paper ruled in $\frac{1}{4}$ in squares

Tracing paper

Piece of thin cardboard at least 7 in square

Ruler

Yardstick

Fabric-marking pencil or pen

Craft knife

Masking tape

Quilting hoop (optional)

Sewing equipment and threads

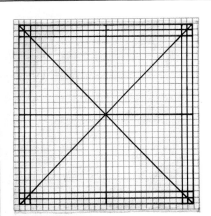

1 Dividing the 6$\frac{1}{2}$ in square into 8 equal sections

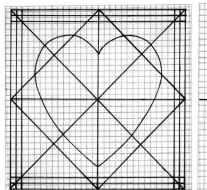

2 Tracing the heart shape and diamond shape onto the square

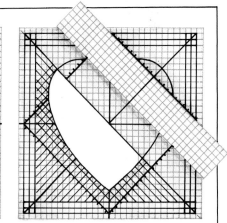

3 Marking the guidelines for the quilting. The darkened center line on the strip is aligned with the principal diagonal line on the pattern

Trace pattern for heart shape

Continue in this way until you have marked 5 rows of 4 motifs each.

9 Using a yardstick, mark 2 more lines around the whole design, the first $\frac{1}{4}$ in from the edge and the second $\frac{3}{8}$ in from the first. This outer line will serve as a guide for the binding. Join the dots at the edge of each square to complete the intersecting borders that run through the design.

10 Press the remaining piece of the main fabric and lay it, wrong side up, on a flat surface. Place the batting, and then the marked fabric, on top. Pin, then baste the layers together as shown in steps 2 and 3, page 13. Mount the work, centered, in a quilting hoop (optional).

11 Using the coton à broder and a crewel needle, work running stitch along the quilting lines, beginning with the main grid lines. In the quilt shown , shades of blue thread are used for the horizontal grid lines and shades of turquoise for the vertical ones – the darkest shades being used for the center lines. Violet is used to outline the heart shapes, and the various patterns are worked in assorted colors.

12 When the quilting is complete, remove all basting except for the line around the edges.

Binding

1 From the patterned fabric, cut and join enough 2 in-wide bias strips (see page 166) to make a strip 125 in long. Beginning at one corner, pin the binding along the top of the quilt, right side down, with one raw edge aligned with the outer marked lines ($\frac{3}{8}$ in from the outer line of quilting). Baste and machine stitch the binding in place, mitering the corners (see page 167).

2 Trim the excess fabric, turn the binding to the wrong side, and slipstitch it in place.

TIED CRIB QUILT

Rich, subtle colors are used for this simple quilt, in which the layers are tied together. You could use the same basic design and silk fabrics to make a luxurious quilt for an adult's bed.

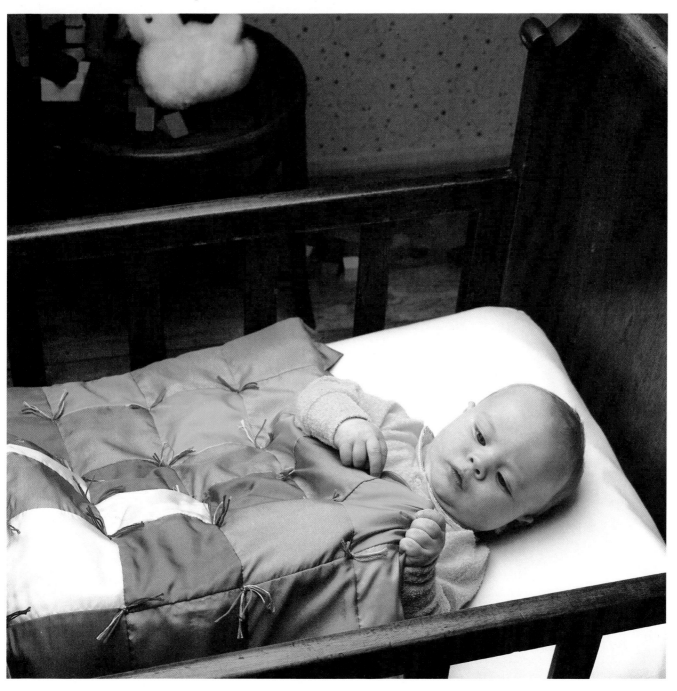

Size
approximately 30 in by 38 in

You will need:
6 different shades of 45 in-wide lustrous polyester fabric in the following amounts:

turquoise, ⅜ yd

mauve, ⅜ yd

terra cotta, ⅜ yd

peach, ⅜ yd

cream, ¼ yd

cinnamon, ¼ yd

1¼ yd of one of the above fabrics for lining and edging

Piece of thick polyester batting, 28½ in by 39 in

1 skein each of embroidery thread (stranded floss, pearl cotton, or coton à broder) in at least 3 colors

Chenille needle, size 19 or 20

Cardboard

Right-angled triangle

Steel ruler

Craft knife

Fabric marking pen

Sewing equipment and threads

1 Make a cardboard template 5 in square (see page 52). Use it to cut squares from the various fabrics as follows: turquoise, 13; mauve, 14; cream, 8; terra cotta, 12; peach, 12; cinnamon, 4.
2 From the fabric used for lining cut a piece 28½ in wide and 39 in long. Also cut 52 squares measuring 3¼ in for the edging.
3 Join the squares in rows, following the diagram on page 29 and taking ⅜ in seam allowance. Press the seam allowances to one side, for extra strength. Then join the rows to complete the patchwork.
4 Prepare the squares for the edging: fold each in half diagonally and press, then fold again and press, as shown in step 1 below.
5 Place the triangles on the patchwork as shown in step 2 below, matching raw edges and overlapping the triangles ¾ in. Baste them in place.
6 Place the patchwork right side up on the batting, then lay the lining, wrong side up, on top. Pin the layers together and baste around the edges as shown in step 3 below.
7 Machine stitch through all layers, ⅜ in from the edge, leaving a 12 in opening along one side. Trim the batting close to the stitching line and trim the fabric corners. Turn the quilt right side out. Slipstitch the opening edges.
8 Working outward from the center, pin the layers together at each intersection of the squares.
9 Thread the chenille needle with a mixture of 3 embroidery threads and tie the layers together as shown on page 29, leaving ends of about 1 in to 1½ in as desired.

Making a zigzag edging

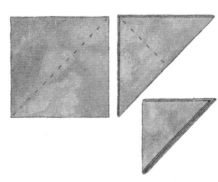

1 *Fold small squares of fabric twice diagonally (pressing each fold) to form triangles.*

2 *Pin and baste the triangles to the right side of the work, matching raw edges and overlapping the triangles as shown.*

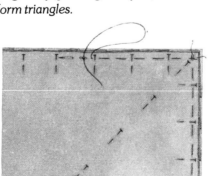

3 *Baste the lining to the patchwork, right sides facing, enclosing the border triangles.*

Tufting or tying

Tufting or tying is a quick and effective alternative to quilting which is often used on patchwork quilts. Use a thick, non-synthetic thread such as crochet cotton, and a chenille needle, and make evenly-spaced knots at intervals of about 6 in across the patchwork. Often the position of the knots is suggested by the design of the quilt.

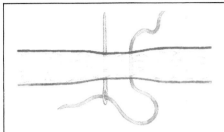
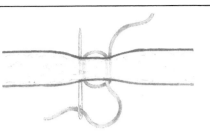
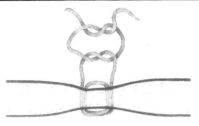

1 *Take the needle down through all layers, leaving a short end, then bring it up a short distance to one side.*

2 *Repeat step 1, pulling gently to bring the layers together.*

3 *Tie the ends in a double knot and trim them to the desired length. Several strands of thread may be used, if desired.*

Piecing diagram for the crib quilt

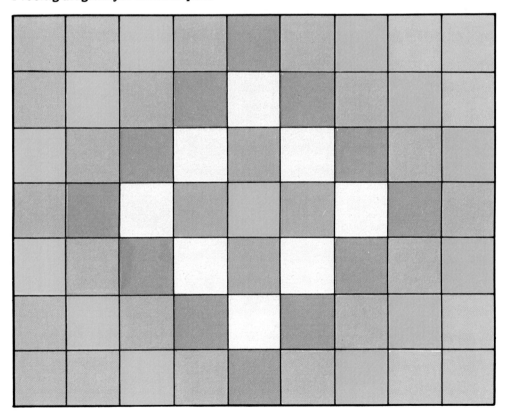

MACHINE QUILTING

Using a machine for quilting has the obvious advantage of being quicker than quilting by hand. And, of course, the stitches will all be even. Another advantage is that you have more scope in your choice of materials. Many synthetic fabrics that are difficult to sew can easily be quilted by machine, and because the line formed is solid, it will show up more easily than running stitch on dark, printed, and textured fabrics. It is also possible to use thicker batting for machine work.

A machine does, however, have its limitations. It cannot easily be used for a large item such as a quilt, for the work will not fit under the body of the machine when the center area is being quilted. (An alternative is to construct the work in blocks which can be quilted individually.) Also, it is not suited to quilting intricate designs, especially those with curved lines, which entail a great deal of turning.

For lattice-type patterns, however, a machine is ideal. Many machines can be fitted with a quilter guide bar, a simple attachment that makes it possible to stitch parallel lines without having to mark them. A twin needle, available for some machines, produces a double line of stitching. For some work an ordinary zigzag stitch can be used.

The methods of marking the fabric and assembling the layers are basically the same as for hand quilting. However, you should take care, when basting, that the stitches do not cover the lines of the design, since they might get caught in the machine stitching and be difficult to remove.

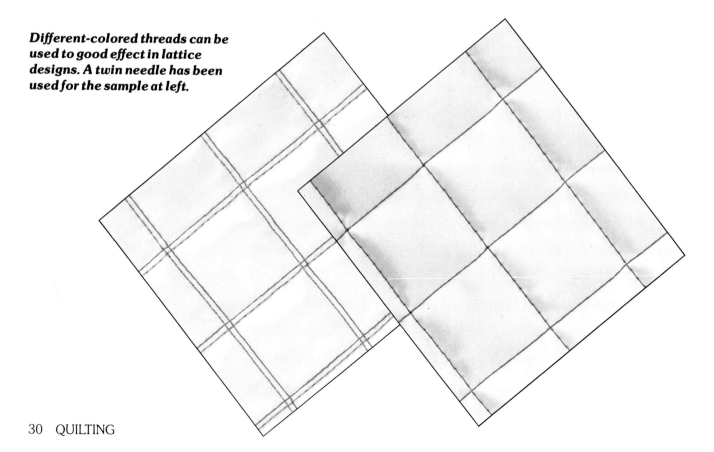

Different-colored threads can be used to good effect in lattice designs. A twin needle has been used for the sample at left.

Before beginning to quilt the design, always test the stitch length and tension on a sample made up of the fabrics and batting being used, and adjust the machine or change the thread if necessary.

Fabrics Although you have a wider choice of fabrics for machine quilting than for hand quilting, you will find the work easiest if you choose one that is closely woven, since the tension produced by quilting can separate loosely-woven threads. If you are in doubt about a fabric's suitability, buy ¼ yd of it and test it on the machine.

Thread Use ordinary cotton-polyester thread in both needle and bobbin. Silk thread can be used in the needle for a lustrous effect.

Needle A size 70 or 80 needle is suitable for lightweight fabrics, size 80 or 90 for medium-weight fabrics. Make sure that the needle is in good condition; a blunt needle can damage the fabric as well as spoil the effect of the stitching.

A quilter guide bar (see below) is useful for stitching parallel lines. If your machine is not designed to take a quilter guide bar, it may still be possible to use one. Loosen the screw that holds the presser foot in place, insert the quilter guide, and tighten the screw; this should hold it securely enough.

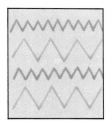

Zigzag stitch makes an interesting alternative to straight stitch quilting.

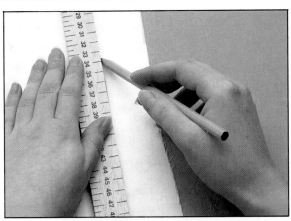

1 Marking the fabric Use one of the marking methods described on page 12. Or, if you are using a quilter guide, draw the first line as shown here. Remember to leave a generous seam allowance. Assemble the layers and baste them together as described in steps 2 and 3, page 13.

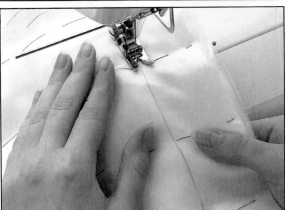

2 Stitching Set the machine for the desired stitch length: about 15 stitches per inch is usually best for a delicate fabric, 10 to 12 stitches per inch for a medium-weight fabric. Stich along the marked line. (Always test the stitching on a sample first.) The quilter guide is attached to the foot, but is not used for the first line.

3 Using the quilter guide Adjust the quilter guide to the desired distance between lines. Place the foot on the fabric with the guide on the first line of stitching and stitch the second line. Continue in this way until you reach the center, then start at the other edge and work toward the center again. This avoids having too much material under the machine at any time.

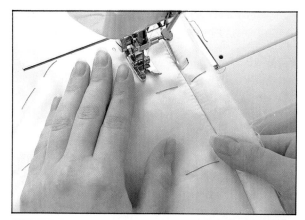

4 Crossing lines Remove the basting before quilting any lines that cross the first ones. To ensure that they are at right angles to the first set of lines, use a right-angled triangle when marking the first line. Quilt the subsequent lines as in step 3.

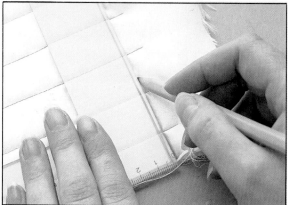

5 Trimming To reduce bulk, trim the batting close to the stitching. Trim the other seam allowances as required for finishing the work.

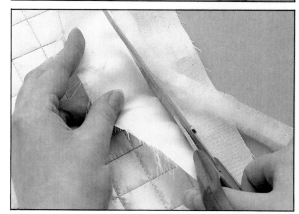

MACHINE-QUILTED BEDROOM PILLOWS

These satin pillows lend a touch of luxury to the bedroom. They're easily quilted by machine, using either the square pattern shown here or one of the alternative patterns given on page 34. Or you could design your own pattern.

Size

approximately 16 in square, excluding the ruffle

You will need:

1 yd of 36 in-wide satin

½ yd of 36 in-wide unbleached muslin

Piece of lightweight batting, 18 in square

Extra-fine cotton-polyester thread, one or two shades darker than the fabric

Quilter guide bar (optional)

Ruler

Right-angled triangle

Fabric-marking pencil

Pillow form 16 in square

Sewing equipment and threads

Working the quilting

1 From the satin fabric cut 2 pieces, each 18 in square, across the width of the fabric. From the remaining fabric cut 4 strips, also across the width, each 36 in by 3½ in.

2 From the muslin backing fabric, cut one piece 18 in square. (If you wish to quilt both sides of the pillow you will need another piece of backing and another of the batting.)

3 Using the ruler and marking pencil, draw the first quilting line 1⅜ in from one edge of one satin square. Make sure that it runs exactly parallel to the edge. (If you are not using a quilter guide bar, mark all the lines.)

4 Assemble the three layers – backing, batting, and satin – and pin and baste them together as shown in steps 2 and 3, page 13.

5 Machine stitch along the marked line. Then set the quilter guide to ⅞ in and stitch parallel to the first line, keeping the guide on the first line of stitching (see step 3, page 32). Continue until you have stitched 9 lines.

6 Remove the fabric from the machine. Measure off 7 in from the center line and mark another line, parallel to the opposite edge. Quilt along this line, then quilt the remaining 7 lines at ⅞ in intervals, working toward the center as before.

7 Work 17 lines of quilting at right angles to the first. When marking the first line, check with the triangle to make sure it forms a 90° angle to the others. Quilt from the sides to the center, as before.

8 Trim the batting close to the stitching on all four sides.

Assembling the pillow

1 Join the four ruffle strips, taking ½ in seam allowance. Press the seams open and finish them if necessary. Turn up and stitch a double ¼ in hem on one long edge. On the other edge stitch 2 rows of gathering stitches.

2 Pull up the gathering threads so that the ruffle measures approximately 65 in. Pin the ruffle to the other satin square, with wrong side of ruffle to right side of satin and raw edges together, placing the seams in the middle of each side. Distribute the fullness evenly and pull up the gathers, if necessary, to fit the edge. Baste around the sides. Secure the thread ends with a pin.

3 Place the quilted piece on top, right side down, on top of the other piece and baste around the edges, taking care not to catch in the folds of the ruffle. Stitch ½ in from the edge, leaving a 10 in gap in one side. Grade the seam allowances and turn the cover right side out.

4 Insert the pillow form. Slipstitch the opening edges together.

Two alternative quilting designs for the pillows

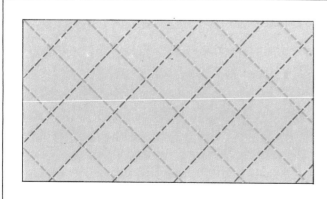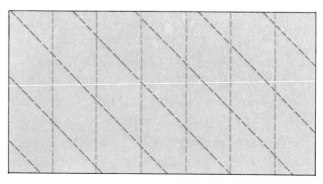

TIGER SLEEPING BAG

This engaging bedtime companion is made of stripes of bright-colored fabric enclosing thick strips of batting. The head contains a pillow. Apart from the embroidery on the face, it is made entirely by machine. You can vary the basic design by using one of the alternative animal characters shown on pages 38-39.

Size

approximately 58 in from head to foot and 29 in wide

You will need:

$3\frac{3}{8}$ yd of 45 in wide dark brown cotton polyester fabric

$1\frac{3}{4}$ yd of rust-colored cotton-polyester fabric, any width

$1\frac{3}{4}$ yd of beige cotton-polyester fabric, any width

$1\frac{3}{4}$ yd of striped cotton-polyester fabric, any width

$\frac{1}{2}$ yd of black cotton-polyester fabric, any width

Small scrap of yellow fabric

$2\frac{1}{2}$ yd of thick polyester batting

Scraps of lightweight polyester batting

4 yd of 1 in-wide single fold bias tape

36 in heavy duty zipper

1 skein of black stranded embroidery floss

Crewel needle, size 5

18 in diameter round pillow form

1 yd each of black and cream cotton fringe

Tracing paper

Graph paper

Sewing equipment and threads

Cutting out

1 Enlarge the patterns for head, ears, and paws given on page 37, as indicated (see page 167). adding $\frac{1}{4}$ in seam allowance to the paw and ear. Trace the eyes (all three pieces), nose, and muzzle.

2 From the dark brown fabric cut the following pieces: 1 piece 45 in by 59 in for the inside of the bag; 2 pieces 4 in by 59 in for stripes, 2 tail pieces 4 in by 5 in, 2 head pieces, 4 paws, 2 ears, and the muzzle.

3 From the black fabric cut the following pieces: 4 paws, 2 ears, the nose, 2 outer eye shapes, and 2 pupils.

4 From the beige fabric cut 5 pieces $4\frac{3}{4}$ in by 59 in, 4 pieces $4\frac{3}{4}$ in by 36 in, and 2 tail pieces 4 in by 5 in.

5 From the rust fabric cut 4 pieces $4\frac{3}{4}$ in by 59 in, 4 pieces $4\frac{3}{4}$ in by 36 in, and 2 tail pieces 4 in by 5 in.

6 From the striped fabric cut 4 pieces $3\frac{1}{2}$ in by 59 in and 6 pieces $3\frac{1}{2}$ in by 36 in.

7 From the batting cut 15 pieces $3\frac{1}{4}$ in by 59 in, and 14 pieces $3\frac{1}{4}$ in by 36 in.

8 Cut the irises from the scrap of yellow fabric.

Stitching and quilting

1 Place one beige strip on the piece of brown fabric, wrong sides together and long edges matching. Pin these outer edges together, turning in $\frac{1}{2}$ in, then topstitch close to the edges.

2 Place a strip of batting under the beige strip and pin the fabric over it. Pin a rust strip on top of the beige, right sides facing and raw edges matching. Stitch through all three thicknesses, taking $\frac{5}{8}$ in seam allowance.

3 Place another strip of batting on the fabric and turn the rust strip over it. Add a striped fabric strip and stitch as in step 2. Continue in this way, adding strips in the order shown in the photograph, until you reach the edge of the brown fabric. Enclose the last strip of batting, joining the fabric edges as in step 1.

4 Bind the raw edges of the bag with the bias tape, placing the tape, with the edge unfolded, on the striped side of the bag and machine stitching along the crease, then taking it to the underside and hand-sewing the folded edge over the stitching line.

5 Fold the bag in half crosswise. Pin and baste the bound edges over the zipper, placing it about 1 in down from the top. Slipstitch the zipper in place, using strong thread. Join the remaining seam to the bottom edge.

6 Pin a black and a brown paw piece together, right sides facing. Stitch $\frac{1}{4}$ in from the edge, leaving the straight edge open. Clip the curves, turn the paw right side out, and press. Stitch straight lines on the paw as indicated on the pattern. Stuff the paw lightly with bits of batting. Turn in the raw edges and stitch them together. Make the remaining three paws in the same way.

7 Position 2 of the paws on the body (see photograph) and slipstitch them in place. Baste the other paws to the back lower edge of the body.

8 To make the tail, seam the tail pieces together along their 4 in edges, alternating the fabrics as shown. Press the seams open and fold the tail lengthwise, right sides facing. Stitch along the edge and across the bottom, tapering the seam to curve the end. Turn the tail right side out and stuff it with bits of batting. Turn under the raw edges and stitch across the top.

9 Baste the tail to the lower edge of the bag, between the paws. Baste the bag edges together, enclosing the paws and tail, and stitch over the existing line of stitching.

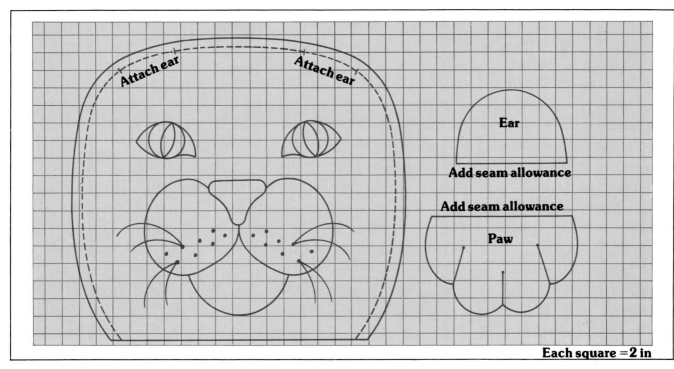

Each square = 2 in

10 On one of the brown head pieces mark a vertical line down the center. Place a strip of batting over the line, then lay a striped piece on top, pinning the edges over the batting. Join a rust strip to each side, and quilt the face as for the body, alternating the fabrics as shown.

11 Quilt the back of the head in the same way.

12 Stitch bias binding to the neck edge of each piece, right sides facing, then turn the binding to the underside so that the seam is on the edge. Hand sew the tape to the lining.

13 Assemble the ears as for the paws (see step 6, above), and baste them to the inside edge of the back head piece.

14 Pin and baste the nose and muzzle to the face. Work close zigzag stitch around the outer edges, leaving a small gap on the chin. Insert small pieces of lightweight batting, cut to shape, then stitch along the remaining edges and the lines of the muzzle.

15 Assemble the pieces for the eyes, then zigzag stitch them to the face.

16 Using all six strands of the embroidery floss, work French knots on the muzzle as shown. Embroider the whiskers using stem stitch.

17 Place the two head pieces together with right sides facing. Pin, baste, and stitch them together, taking $\frac{5}{8}$ in seam allowance. Trim the seam allowances and finish them together with zigzag. Turn the head right side out.

18 Place the head on the opened bag, with the face against the inside back and the straight edges even. Baste the front neck edge to the bag, then overcast the edges together, spacing the stitches closely, but not working too deeply into the fabric. Cut the two lengths of fringe in half.

19 Pin the brown fringe on top of the cream fringe, so that the latter extends slightly beyond the former, and machine stitch them together. Slipstitch the fringe to the head as shown in the photograph, just in front of the seam.

20 Insert the pillow form into the head. Turn under the straight edge of the back of the head. Pin, baste, and stitch the edge in place.

French knots

Bring the needle up at the point for the knot; wind the thread once or twice around the needle; then insert the needle next to the point where it emerged and draw the thread through quickly.

Stem stitch

Bring the needle up at the beginning of the stitching line, then take it down about $\frac{1}{4}$ in along the line; bring it up halfway between these two points; repeat.

QUILTED MENAGERIE

Here are some more ideas for original animal sleeping bags.

1

2

3

1 *For a panda, join narrow lengths of black and white brushed acrylic. Machine quilt after assembling fabric and batting.*

1

2 *For a pink elephant, use cotton satin covered with a layer of net and quilt in random swirling lines as shown. Add a net tutu for fun.*

3 For a koala bear, use brushed acrylic fabric. Tie the layers together with bouclé yarn. Make yarn loops for the ears.

4 For a lion, join two shades of bright orange terry cloth and machine quilt along the seams. Work loops of thick rug yarn for the mane and the tail switch.

5 For a tabby cat, use two-color striped fabric and quilt along selected lines.

QUILTING 39

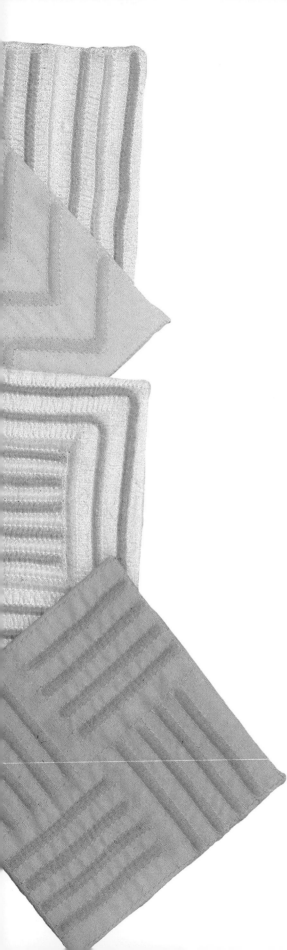

ITALIAN QUILTING

Also called "corded quilting," this form of quilting is purely decorative. It consists of stitching two layers of fabric together with a double line of stitching, forming channels which are then filled with cord or yarn to produce a raised line on the fabric. The technique can be used to form free-style motifs or geometric patterns. It can be worked entirely as a relief design, using opaque fabric, or as shadow work, using a sheer fabric on top and threading colored cords through the channels.

Italian quilting is ideal for adding a little textural and linear interest to a fabric. It makes an attractive detail around the hem of a skirt or the edges of a boxy vest, for example. It can be used to decorate household accessories, such as pillows and curtains. Designs for Italian quilting can be fairly complex, including interlaced curved lines. However, attractive patterns can be made using only straight lines, as the bedspread on page 45 illustrates.

Such simple designs can be marked directly on the fabric (see step 1, page 41) using a ruler. Depending on the desired width of the channel, it may be possible to mark only one line and use the presser foot as a guide when stitching the other. If the design is at all complex, however, you should draw it on a sheet of paper, including both lines, and then transfer the design to the fabric using the pricking method shown on page 12.

Fabrics The top fabric for Italian quilting should be soft and pliable, but not stretchy; China silk, satin, poplin, chambray, cotton broadcloth and lightweight linen are among the possibilities.

A loosely-woven fabric such as muslin should be used for the backing if the design is complex, as it will need to be cut in places when pulling the yarn through the channel.

Fillings Yarn is often used to fill the channels. Experiment with different thicknesses of yarn and different widths of channel to get the desired effect. Cotton filler cord is a good choice; it comes in a variety of thicknesses and gives a firm outline. Always pre-shrink it before use. Colored decorative cord can be used to good effect with a sheer top fabric. Remember that the color of the filler cord or yarn will be softened by the fabric.

Sewing equipment The design is normally stitched by machine, using ordinary sewing thread; but you can, instead, sew by hand using quilting thread and backstitch, for a solid line. For inserting the yarn or cord you will need a bodkin. Sharp dressmaker's scissors are required for cutting the fabric; embroidery scissors are needed if the backing must be snipped.

To estimate the amount of cord you will need, measure the lines of the design, multiplying as appropriate. Add about 3 in-4 in extra per yard for shrinkage. If you are using knitting yarn, you will probably need only one ball, unless the work is extensive.

Materials for transferring designs A ruler or yardstick and a fabric marking pencil or pen will be needed for marking a straight-line design. For a more complex one, requiring the pricking method, you will need a sheet of paper, powder, and a felt pad.

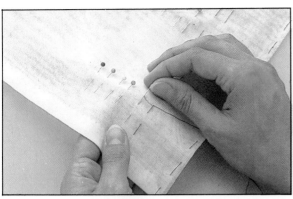

1 Marking Cut the two fabrics to the desired size, plus seam allowance. Allow a little extra for the shrinkage caused by the quilting. Join the side seams (unless they will be bound), leaving openings for the channels. Mark the design lines on the top fabric, then pin and baste the fabrics together, basting close to the marked lines.

2 Stitching Using a small to medium-length stitch and matching or contrasting thread, stitch directly on the marked lines to form the channels for the yarn or cord.

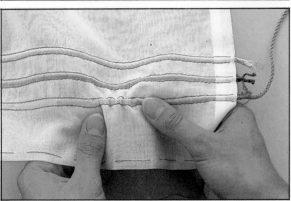

3 Inserting the filler Thread the yarn or cord into the bodkin and anchor the loose end to the main strand with a few stitches. Push the bodkin and yarn through the channels. (If the design is intricate, you will need to cut little slits in the backing at turning points, pull the yarn through, then re-insert it.)

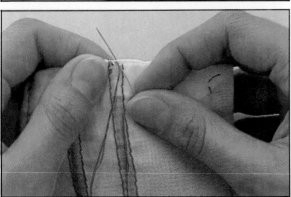

4 Fastening off Sew through the ends of the cord a few times to prevent unraveling, then cut them off just beyond this point. Push the end back into the channel and close the opening by hand. Or, if the edge will be bound, stitch over the cords within the seam allowance, to hold them in place.

1

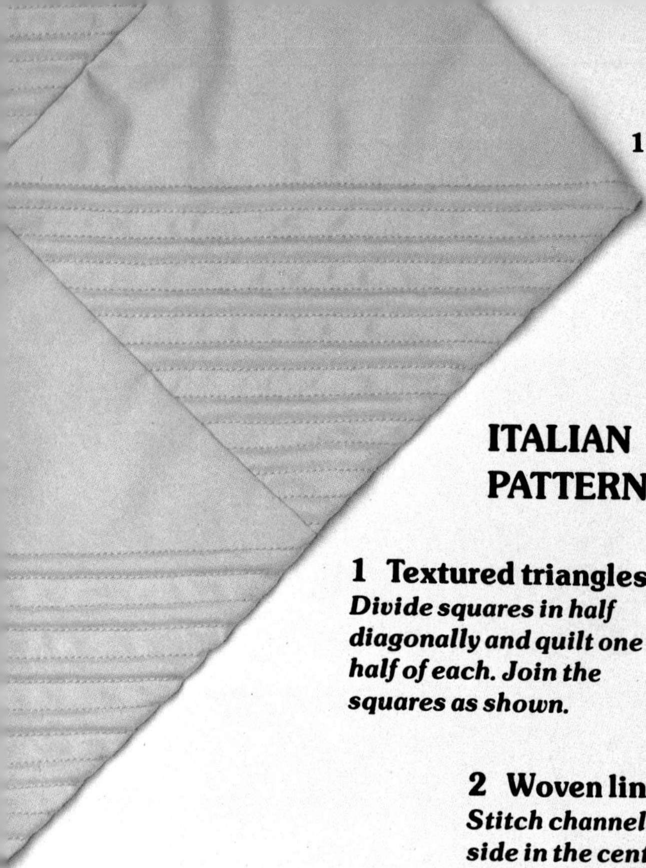

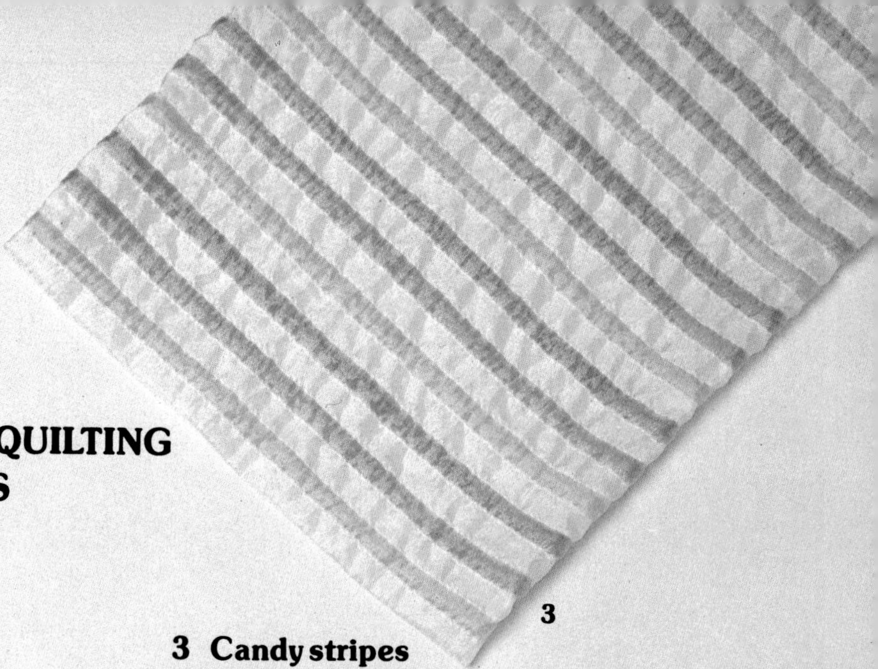

ITALIAN QUILTING PATTERNS

1 Textured triangles
Divide squares in half diagonally and quilt one half of each. Join the squares as shown.

2 Woven lines
Stitch channels side by side in the center of a square and insert yarn or cord in each. Join the squares as shown.

3 Candy stripes
Use voile, organdy, or sheer silk for the top fabric and opaque fabric for the backing. Insert bright-colored yarn in the channels.

4 Basketweave
Space the quilting lines evenly across each square and alternate the direction of the finished quilting as shown.

3

2

4

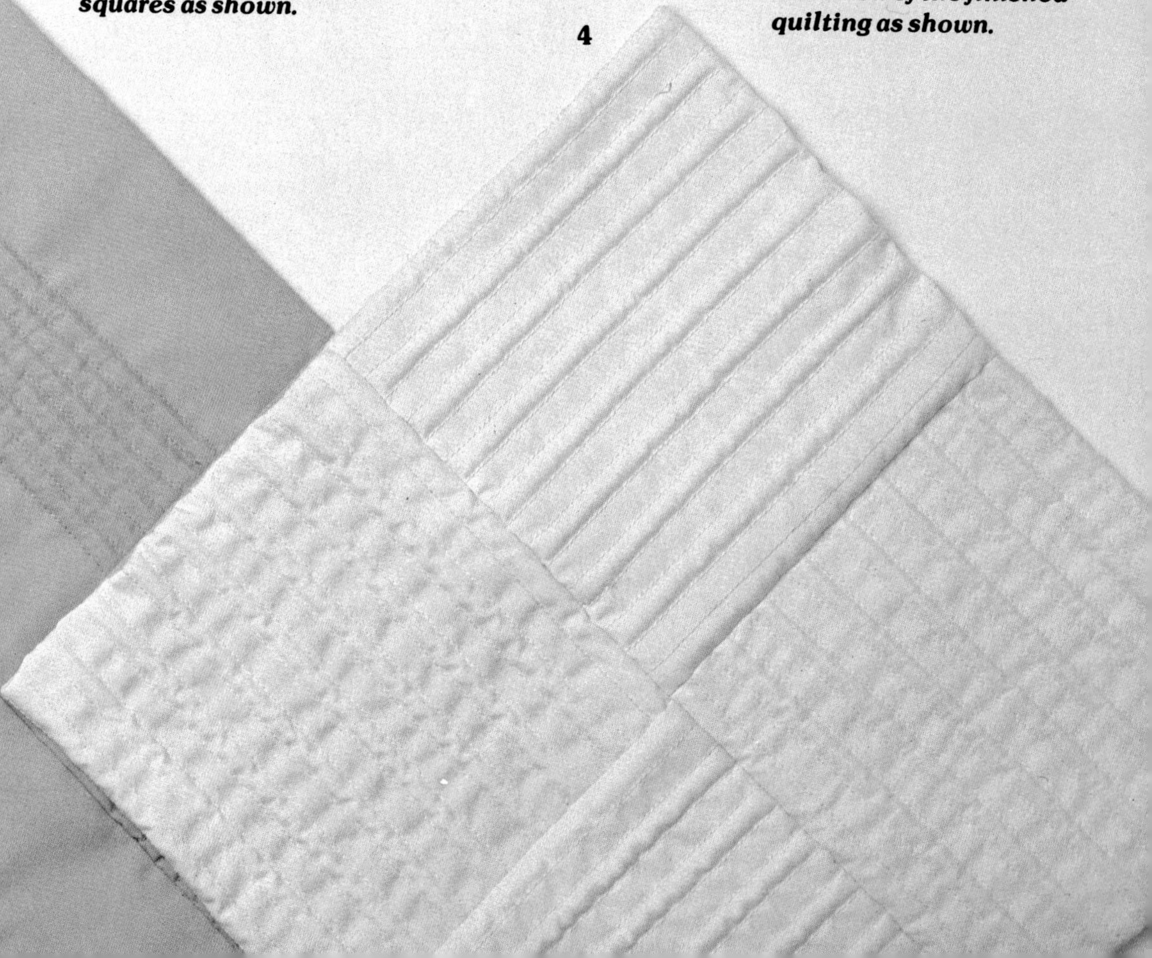

ITALIAN-QUILTED CAFE CURTAIN

Bright-colored cords are used for the Italian quilting on this crisp café curtain, which looks as good from the outside as from inside.

You will need:

1¼ yd of 60 in-wide sheer white curtain fabric, such as marquisette

1¾ yd of ⅛ in-diameter decorative rayon cord in each of 3 colors

3½ yd of ⅛ in-diameter decorative rayon cord in white

Bodkin

Fabric-marking pencil

Piece of thin cardboard

Sewing equipment and threads

Attaching the cord to the wrong side of the curtain with zigzag stitch. A contrasting thread is used here only for clarity.

1 Fold the fabric in half crosswise (wrong sides facing if there is a wrong side). Pin and baste the side edges together. Mark the positions for the quilting, 2 in, 3 in, and 4 in up from the folded edge, allowing a generous ¼ in for each channel. Stitch the side seams, omitting the spaces left for the channels. Trim the seams and finish them together with zigzag stitch.

2 Turn the curtain right side out. Baste the layers together close to the fold to prevent them from slipping. Measure and mark the lines for the quilting, using a fabric-marking pencil and yardstick. Pin and baste the fabrics together along the lines. Machine stitch along the basted lines to form the channels for the cord. (See steps 1 and 2, page 41).

3 Thread each cord into a bodkin (see step 3, page 41), and insert it into one of the channels. Secure the cord ends as shown in step 4, page 41.

4 On the cardboard make a template for the scalloped upper edge of the curtain: draw a straight line 5¾ in long, then, using a saucer as a guide, draw a curved line connecting the two ends. Cut out the template.

5 Pin the upper edges of the curtain together. Using the yardstick and fabric-marking pencil, mark the seamline, ½ in from the edge, on one side. Place the template on this line and mark around the curved edge, beginning at one corner and leaving ¼ in between each marked curve.

6 Turn the curtain wrong side out. Pin the edges together again and baste around the curves, just inside the marked line (which should be visible). Machine stitch, leaving one scallop in the center open for turning. Trim the fabric a scant ¼ in from the stitching line; clip the curves.

7 Turn the curtain right side out. Turn in the edges of the opening, and baste and slipstitch them together.

8 Measure the circumference of your curtain rod. Then stitch the white cord to the underside of the scalloped edge, using a wide zigzag stitch, as shown at left, (but using matching thread) and forming a loop at each point about ¾ in longer than the circumference of the rod. Hand sew over the ends of cord to prevent them from raveling.

ITALIAN-QUILTED BEDSPREAD

This elegant bedspread is made of silky poplin and quilted with a sophisticated pattern of diagonal corded lines.

Size
approximately 65 in by 75 in

You will need:
9 yd of 45 in-wide cotton-polyester poplin

Approximately 350 yd of soft bulky yarn

Bodkin

Graph paper ruled in 1 in squares

Dressmaker's carbon paper

Ruler

Yardstick

Fabric-marking pencil

Sewing equipment and threads

Quilting the panels
1 Cut the fabric crosswise into 4 lengths, each measuring 80 in. Now cut the following pieces from the 80 in length: 12 pieces 9 in wide for the main panels, 10 pieces 4 in wide for panel bands, 2 pieces 6¼ in wide for side bands. Also cut 2 pieces 70 in long and 6¼ in wide for top and bottom bands.

2 Using the graph paper, enlarge the design given on page 47 (see page 167).

3 Using dressmaker's carbon paper, transfer the design to 3 of the 9 in-wide panels. Use a ruler and hard pencil or ball-point pen to ensure straight, firm lines. Position the top line of the design 2 in from the upper edge of the fabric. Reverse the design and trace it onto 3 more 9 in-wide panels. (If the lines are not visible on the wrong side of the paper, darken them with a felt tip pen.)

4 Pin and baste each of the 6 marked panel pieces to one of the unmarked panel pieces, with wrong sides together.

5 Before beginning to quilt the panels, cut 2 swatches of fabric, baste them together, and work several parallel lines of machine stitching, approximately ¼ in to ⅜ in apart, to see which width is best suited to the yarn you are using.

6 Starting at the top of a panel, machine stitch along the first marked line. Then stitch a second line below it, the correct distance, as established in step 5. Continue stitching parallel lines to complete the design.

7 Thread the bodkin with a length of yarn long enough for several channels. Insert this into the first channel. Trim the ends at each side to about 1 in. Repeat to fill the remaining channels, re-threading the bodkin when necessary.

8 Quilt the remaining five panels in the same way.

Adding the strips
1 In the center of 5 of the 4 in wide strips, mark off (along each narrow edge) 7 spaces, each the width of the quilting channels. Baste each of these marked strips to an unmarked strip, wrong sides together.

2 Mark the first stitching line in from one edge, using the fabric-marking pencil and a yardstick. Stitch along this line, then stitch the remaining 7 parallel lines.

3 Thread lengths of yarn through the center 3 channels as shown on page 41. Repeat steps 10 and 11 on the other 4 strips.

4 Place a strip on one of the panels, with right sides facing and edges matching. Pin and baste, then stitch, with the strip on top, to form another channel, while joining the seam. Repeat to join all the strips and panels, alternating the panels so that the quilting lines converge as shown in the diagram.

5 Thread lengths of yarn through the channels formed in the seaming. Trim the crosswise lengths of yarn close to the seam by pushing the fabric back and then cutting.

6 Trim the seam allowances on the strips to ¼ in. Fold the seam allowance on the panels over the quilted channel, turning in the raw edge, and slipstitch it neatly to the underside of the quilting.

7 Fold the 6¼ in strips in half lengthwise, wrong sides together, and pin and baste the raw edges. Starting at the folded edge, stitch 8 parallel lines, the same width as in step 9.

8 Starting at the fold, thread the first and the next 3 alternate channels with yarn. Join the strips to the remaining long edges of the bedspread, adding another line of quilting, as in steps 13 and 14.

9 Trim the lower edge of the bedspread to within 1 in of the bottom line of quilting.

10 Fold, stitch, and quilt the top and bottom strips as for the side strips, as in steps 15 and 16, and stitch it to the remaining edges, leaving an equal overlap at each end.

11 Trim the overlapping ends of the strips, if necessary, to 1 in. Trim the ends of the yarn and fold the excess fabric to the underside, turning in the raw edges. Baste and slipstitch these hems in place.

Each square = 1 in

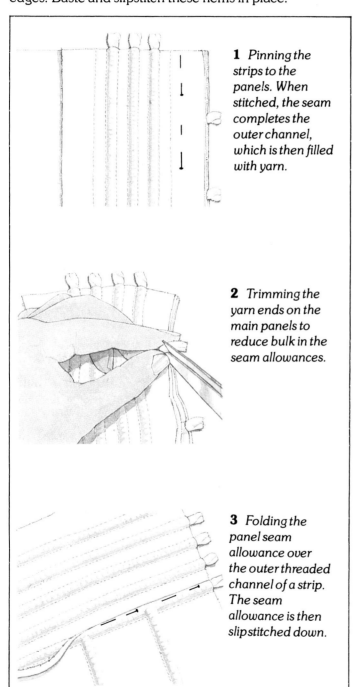

1 *Pinning the strips to the panels. When stitched, the seam completes the outer channel, which is then filled with yarn.*

2 *Trimming the yarn ends on the main panels to reduce bulk in the seam allowances.*

3 *Folding the panel seam allowance over the outer threaded channel of a strip. The seam allowance is then slipstitched down.*

PATCHWORK

Surviving examples of patchwork from earlier times often reflect not only the tastes of those times but also the economy and general environment. For example, the bright printed calicos featured in so much English patchwork of the 17th century reflect the increased trade with India. The fairly simple designs of the patchwork itself gave way, in the following century, to intricate, mosaic-like patterns requiring many hours of painstaking stitching – an indication that patchwork had graduated from being mainly utilitarian to being a pastime for a growing leisured class.

In 19th century America, where patchwork was an essential – if pleasurable – domestic task, the designs were even more intricate than in England, but the method used to join the patches was quicker and simpler. Instead of folding the patches over paper shapes and joining them edge to edge, American patchworkers joined them with ordinary seams. Using squares and triangles almost exclusively and combining small units into progressively larger ones, they devised countless patterns – many of them, such as "Road to California," "Railway Crossing," and "Indian Trail," symbolic of life on the frontier. The influence of Indian art is clearly apparent in many of these designs.

With the revival of interest in patchwork in our own time has come an eagerness to experiment, to combine old and new techniques, and to draw on the traditions of other people. Aided by the profusion of fabrics available today, modern patchworkers have endless creative possibilities at their disposal, and many of them are producing exciting, innovative work.

These projects can be made by adapting the techniques described in the following pages.

PATCHWORK BASICS

Careful planning and accuracy are the key factors in successful patchwork. The sewing involved is not difficult, especially with the aid of a machine. But it is still important to spend plenty of time choosing the right fabrics and marking and cutting them with precision so that they will fit together smoothly.

Designing

For your first attempt at designing patchwork it is best to make something fairly small, such as a throw pillow, which will not require an enormous investment of time. Begin by selecting the shapes. If you are planning a piece of English patchwork (see page 113), this is fairly simple. However, if you are doing block method patchwork, you have an enormous choice. The patterns shown on pages 56-57 are but a few of the hundreds available.

Draw your chosen block to scale on graph paper. Photocopy it or redraw it several times so that you will have extra copies to work on. Next, using colored pencils, fill in the sections of the block to establish different tonal values. Color several blocks, changing the pattern of light and dark in each.

When you have found an arrangement that pleases you, draw a group of four of these blocks to see how the pattern works in repetition. If you don't like the effect, try separating the blocks with strips or solid blocks.

Once you have worked out your design, you can choose fabrics in which to interpret it. You need not, of course, stick to your original color scheme. The important thing is to maintain the balance of light and dark tones. The use of patterned fabrics often helps to achieve contrasts, although the successful use of many different prints requires a practiced eye. In general, small prints are best; larger ones may detract from the lines of the patchwork.

If possible, buy small amounts of a selection of fabrics before making your final decision. Cut trial patches and arrange them in your chosen pattern. Try different arrangements until you are completely satisfied with the effect.

Fabrics for patchwork

Dressweight cottons are the most suitable fabrics for patchwork – now as in the past. They are the easiest fabrics to handle on a machine and are also easily sewn by hand (an important consideration if the work is to be quilted). Because they take a crease well, they are particularly good for patterns with sharply-defined shapes, such as triangles and diamonds. Cotton-polyester blends are a good substitute, although for English patchwork, in which the fabric must be folded over a paper shape, they may be too springy.

Cotton also has the advantage of being washable. However, if the patchwork will be washed, you must first wash all of the fabrics to make sure they are pre-shrunk and colorfast. If the dye does run, immerse the fabric in a large saucepan of water containing a few tablespoons of vinegar, and boil it for a few minutes; this should set the dye. Then wash the fabric again, along with a piece of white fabric; if the dye runs onto the white, the fabric should not be used.

It is also important that the fabric be closely woven, so that it will hold its shape well, and that it not fray easily. Slippery fabrics, such as satin and

Designing with colored pencils (top) and with fabric scraps (above)

velvet, are tricky to handle and should not be used by a beginner. As a general rule, all-synthetic fabrics are best avoided. In any case, they should not be combined with those made of natural fibers, because the high iron temperature needed for cottons would damage the synthetics. It is also best not to mix different weights of fabric in one project; the heavier fabrics will tend to pull the lighter ones out of shape.

Like most rules, the ones outlined here can sometimes be broken. Heavyweight fabrics can often be used for machine patchwork. And if the work is primarily decorative – a wall-hanging, for example – and will be dry-cleaned, it is possible to be more adventurous in the choice of fabrics. Fine silks can be used, as well as other delicate fabrics; a variety of textures and weights can be combined. Iron-on interfacing applied to the wrong side before the patches are cut may give a flimsy fabric the necessary body.

You can use re-cycled fabrics for patchwork, provided you make sure that they are still in good condition. If a fabric tears at all easily, it is a bad bet. Unused scraps left over from other sewing projects can often be incorporated into patchwork; many attractive quilts use a miscellany of patterned fabrics in a random arrangement; these are called "scrap quilts." Even here, however, it is usually best to make the dominant patches from one or two fabrics, repeated consistently, in order to unify the effect.

Estimating fabric amounts

When you are planning an original design, you must calculate the amount of each fabric that you will need. First count the number of times a given patch of a given fabric is used within one block. Multiply this number by the number of blocks. Divide the width of the fabric by the width of the patch – including seam allowances – to get the number of patches that will fit across the width. Divide the total number of patches required by this number to get the number of rows of patches to be cut. Finally, multiply this figure by the depth of the patch, again including seam allowances. This is the amount of fabric you will need. If many patches are involved, add at least ¼ yd to allow for error. Repeat these calculations for all other patches and fabrics. A sample plan for estimating fabric requirements is shown below.

Borders, if any, may need to be pieced on a large item such as a quilt. However, if the border fabric is also used for much of the patchwork, it may be possible to cut long strips along the lengthwise grain, using the remaining width of fabric for patches.

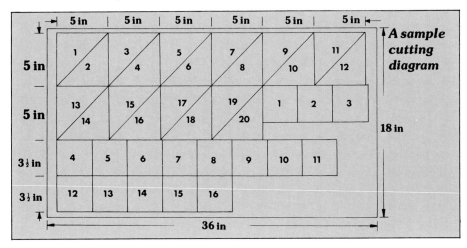

A sample cutting diagram

Lining or backing fabric for a quilt must usually be joined down the middle to make up the necessary width. When you have established the finished size of the quilt, measure the length (including seam allowances) and multiply by 2 (or by 3 if the fabric is narrow and the quilt wide) to get the amount to buy.

Batting for quilts is sold in various widths. In some cases it may be necessary to join widths in order to get a piece of the required size. See page 10 for how to join batting.

Templates

For most patchwork you will need to make your own templates, or patterns, for cutting the patches. It is vital to make sure that these are as accurate as possible, since any error will be repeated time after time and will cause immense problems.

To help ensure accuracy, use the correct materials and equipment. These include some stiff cardboard and a craft knife with replaceable blades for cutting it, a steel ruler for ensuring straight lines when marking and cutting, a hard pencil which produces the necessary fine line, and a cutting board to protect the work surface. This can be a piece of plywood, linoleum, cork, or simply extra-heavy cardboard.

Sheets of graph paper are useful for drawing patterns containing right angles and also for scaling up designs. Tracing paper is used for tracing patterns given in books. The graph pattern or tracing is then glued to the cardboard and the template cut along its edges. In some cases you may also need one or more of the following: a right-angled triangle, a compass for drawing circles and curves and also for hexagons (see page 114), and a protractor for measuring angles.

If you are working with a curved shape, such as a clamshell, and are not experienced in the use of a craft knife, you may prefer to cut two identical shapes from thin cardboard, using scissors (and cutting very carefully), then glue the pieces together.

Fine sandpaper is often a good alternative to cardboard, especially when cutting narrow strips, as for log cabin patchwork, for it grips the surface of the fabric and prevents it from slipping.

For each shape in the design you will need an outer template, the size of the finished shape plus seam allowance on all sides. You may also want to make an inner template the exact finished size; this is optional for machine-stitched patchwork but essential for the English method (see page 115). If you are using patterned fabrics you may also want to make a window template (see page 54). In any case, you will need several of each template, for they become worn in use.

Cutting and joining patches

Patches are normally marked on the wrong side of the fabric, using a colored pencil or a pen with washable ink. Whatever you use, make sure that it makes a fine line, so that you can cut accurately.

A good pair of dressmaking scissors is essential.

For joining the patches you will need other basic sewing equipment: a sewing machine in good working order (unless you are doing only hand-sewn patchwork), a steam iron and pressing cloth, cotton-polyester thread in the appropriate colors, sewing needles, a thimble, fine silk pins, embroidery scissors, a seam ripper; and a tape measure.

BLOCK METHOD PATCHWORK

Most American patchwork – now as in the past – is constructed by the block method. In this method, the basic unit of the design is a block (usually square), which is made up of various smaller shapes: squares, rectangles, triangles, and other geometric figures. The completed blocks are then joined, either directly to each other, or with intervening strips of fabric, or to plain squares, forming a checkerboard effect.

When blocks are joined directly, their individual design takes on a new character. The focal point within a block may now take a secondary role, as other shapes are formed at the seams; colors that appeared subdued may assume a stronger role; entirely new patterns may emerge. It is partly because of such transformations that block patterns are so appealing.

The block method can also be adapted for non-repeating designs, such as pictorial patchwork (see page 58). A group of blocks, each containing a different design, can be joined, or a single image can be formed from strips that have first been constructed using the basic joining system.

Fabrics Because block patchwork is normally worked by machine, there is some freedom in the choice of fabrics. Cottons and wools are usually easiest to handle, but natural-synthetic blends, and even some all-synthetic fabrics, can be used successfully. However, you should avoid any fabric that frays easily, that stretches, or that resists pressing. If you are in any doubt about a fabric's suitability, buy a small amount and make up a sample of patchwork to see the effect. This step is particularly important if you are mixing different types of fabric – which, in any case, is not recommended for a beginner.

Templates For block method patchwork you have a choice of methods regarding templates. You can use both an outer and an inner template, for marking the patches and the stitching lines, respectively, as shown in steps 2 and 5, pages 54-55. Or, if you prefer, you can use only an outer template. In this case, you must take care to keep the seam allowances even and uniform throughout. To achieve this, either use the edge of the presser foot as a guide or attach a strip of masking tape to the needle plate the required distance from the needle. The two-template method should be used, however, if you are a beginner or if you are sewing the patchwork by hand.

Sewing equipment If you are sewing the patchwork by machine, you should make sure that the needle is in good condition and that the needle size, stitch length, and tension are suitable for the fabric. Work a sample and make any necessary adjustments. Use cotton-wrapped polyester thread, which is strong and can take a hot iron if necessary. You will also need sharp dressmaker's scissors and some silk pins, which will not mark the fabric.

1 Making templates Draw and cut 2 templates for each shape: an outer template, including seam allowance, and an inner template, the size of the finished patch. Use a steel ruler when marking and when cutting, to steady the craft knife. Pull the craft knife toward you in one smooth movement, taking care to keep your fingers out of the way. (You may want to use different-colored cardboard for the two sets of templates, to avoid confusing them.)

2 Marking the fabric Using the outer templates and working on the wrong side of the fabric, draw around the templates, butting the edges of the shapes. Make sure that the first patch is marked on the straight grain; if so, the others will also lie correctly.

3 Window templates For some printed fabrics it is advisable to use a window template. The inner edge represents the stitching line; the outer edge the cutting line. Position the template on the right side of the fabric to show the pattern to best advantage, still keeping it on the straight grain.

4 Cutting out Cut out the patches using sharp scissors. Check the design to make sure that you have cut the correct number and shapes for each block. Keep all the patches for a block together.

5 Marking stitching lines Center the inner template on the wrong side of a patch and mark around it with a pencil. This marks the stitching line.

6 Joining patches Pin two adjacent patches together with right sides facing and raw edges matching. The stitching lines should align exactly. If you wish, baste beside the stitching line and remove the pins.

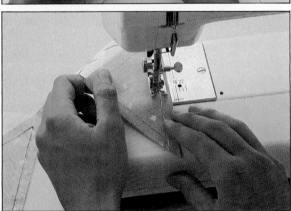

7 Stitching Machine stitch along the stitching line. Remove the basting, if used, and press the seam to one side – preferably toward the darker patch. This makes a stronger joining than pressing the seam open.

8 Completing the patchwork Continue joining patches in the logical order suggested by the design – that is, joining small units to make larger ones. When all the blocks have been made, join the blocks into rows, then join the rows to complete the patchwork.

BLOCK PATTERNS

This selection of some favorite American block patterns includes diagrams showing the construction of each block and its basic shapes, as well as the number of patches in each fabric required for the samples.

1 Square star

This block can be colored many ways to give a variety of designs.

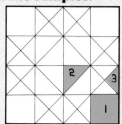

patch 1: 4 of blue and white print

patch 2: 4 of blue; 4 of red, white, and blue print

patch 3: 8 of blue; 8 of red and white stripe; 8 of red, white, and blue print: 8 of blue and white print

2 Cactus basket

There are many different basket patterns. This one — also called Desert or Texas Rose — is an especially interesting one to sew.

patch 1: 4 of red; 4 of violet

patch 2: 2 of green

patch 3: 4 of violet-yellow print (reversible shape)

patch 4: 2 of green print

patch 5: 2 of green print

patch 6: 2 of green print

patch 7: 4 of green print

patch 8: 2 of green

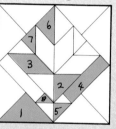

3 T blocks

This widely-used block, also known as Capital T, is suitable where a large-size block is desired.

patch 1: 4 of yellow stripe

patch 2: 8 of emerald green

patch 3: 4 of yellow print, 4 of dark green

patch 4: 8 of dark green; 8 of yellow print; 8 of yellow stripe

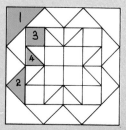

4 Courthouse steps

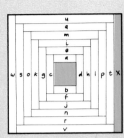

This block is a type of log cabin design (see page 91) and uses two basic shapes: the center square and strips of equal width (but varying length), which are joined in the order shown in the diagram.

4

5

5 Devil's claws

This attractive design is also known as Bright Stars, Cross Plains, and Lily.

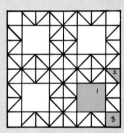

patch 1: 4 of red print
patch 2: 24 of pink; 16 of lilac; 20 of purple; 24 of lilac print; 4 of red print
patch 3: 4 of pink

6

6 Indian Trail

This intricate block is also known as Rambling Road, Forest Path, and Winding Path.

patch 1. 4 of red-black print; 4 of black stripe
patch 2: 4 of red
patch 3: 24 of black; 20 of red print; 4 of red

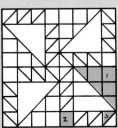

PICTURE PATCHWORK

These variations of the block method are simpler than they may appear. The quilt on page 75 is made using the technique shown in steps 1 and 2.

1 Constructing simple shapes Choose an image that can easily be stylized, and work out the colors and shapes on graph paper, using one square to represent each (square) patch. For diagonal lines, divide squares into triangles. There is no need to draw the design full size; just decide the measurements of each finished square and work out how many you will need lengthwise and crosswise to make the work the desired size. Then fit the design into this framework.

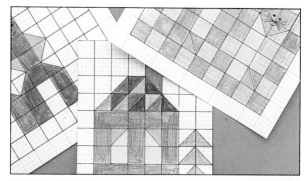

2 Joining the patches Make templates and cut out the patches as usual. Lay out the patches in the correct order. Stitch the patches together row by row, joining triangles into squares first where necessary. Start at the top of the work and join the successive rows together, then join the rows to make one piece.

3 Strip technique This method permits more detail in the picture. First draw the image (outline only) to a reduced scale on graph paper, keeping the lines as straight as possible. Draw a grid of horizontal or vertical, equally-spaced lines over the image. Check that the original outline and any details within it cut through each strip of the grid with a straight line. Color the image, remembering that every color change will entail a seam.

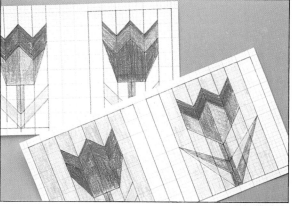

4 Strip templates Enlarge the drawing to the finished size on graph paper (the strips should be at least 1 in wide.) Make a template for each shape by tracing the shape, adding seam allowances as usual, then gluing the tracing to cardboard and cutting it out. To prevent the templates from becoming mixed up, number each shape on the original design and number each template as you cut it out.

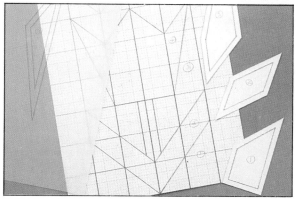

STAR MOTIF PLACEMAT

A selection of small, color-coordinated prints has been used for this attractive quilted placemat. If you wish to make more than one mat, calculate the required amount for each fabric as described in "Estimating fabric amounts," page 51.

Size
approximately 18 in by 12 in

You will need:
(for one mat)

¼ yd each of 5 printed fabrics, any width

⅜ yd of fabric, any width, for backing

Piece of polyester batting 20 in by 14 in

1¾ yd of decorative cord

Cardboard in two different colors

Right-angled triangle

Steel ruler

Craft knife

Fabric-marking pen or pencil

Colored pencils (optional)

Tissue paper (optional)

Sewing equipment and threads

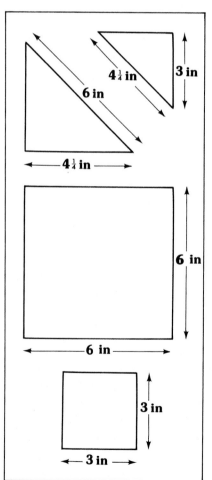

Making the patchwork
1 Plan the arrangement of your fabrics. You can either cut small pieces corresponding to the actual, full-size shapes and try them out or else draw the design and fill in the shapes with colored pencils. (See page 50.)

2 Using the craft knife and steel ruler, draw and cut the inner templates to the measurements shown here.

3 Using the first set of templates as a guide, draw and cut out a set of outer templates from contrasting cardboard, adding ⅜ in seam allowance to each edge. If you are using a medium- or large-scale print for any of the shapes, you may wish to make the corresponding template a window template.

4 Using the larger set of templates and working on the wrong side of the fabric, carefully draw the fabric patches as follows: 1 large square, 8 small squares (4 each of two fabrics), 12 small triangles (4 of one fabric and 8 of another), 6 large triangles (4 of one fabric and 2 of another). Use a window template where necessary, working on the right side of the fabric and marking the outer edge only. Cut out the fabric shapes.

5 Using the smaller set of templates and working on the wrong side of the fabric, mark the stitching line on each piece.

6 Pin, baste (optional), and stitch the patches together as shown in steps 6 and 7, page 55. The suggested sequence of joining is shown in the diagram.

Quilting the placemat
1 Cut the backing fabric to measure the same as the completed patchwork. Turn under ⅜ in on all edges of patchwork and backing and press.

2 Lay the patchwork on top of the batting and baste them together from the center outward to each corner (see page 13).

3 Machine stitch around the center square, right on the seamline. If the batting catches in the machine, place tissue paper underneath it.

4 Trim the batting about ⅛ in in from the pressed edge. Tuck it inside the seam allowance and pin it in place at intervals to secure it.

5 Topstitch all around the mat, about ¼ in from the edge.

6 Pin and baste the backing to the underside of the mat, aligning the folded edges carefully. Topstitch them together, working close to the edges and leaving a 1½ in gap on one of the short sides.

7 Insert one end of the cord into the gap left in the stitching and secure it with a pin. Slipstitch the cord in place around all four edges. Trim the remaining end, if necessary, and tuck it into the gap. Close the edges of the gap and secure the cord ends by hand, as neatly as possible.

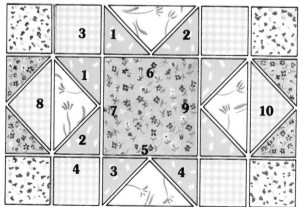

Measurements of templates (far left) and piecing diagram for placemat (left)

STAR MOTIF TABLECLOTH

This square tablecloth, using a subtle mixture of pink and green printed and solid-color fabrics, uses the same motif as is used for the placemat shown on page 59. It is made of 9 pieced blocks. By adding more blocks you could make a larger cloth, a bedspread, or a quilt. A single block – perhaps made of slightly larger pieces – could be used for a pillow cover.

Size

approximately 36 in square

You will need:

7 different fabrics, each 36 in wide, in the following amounts:

Fabric A, $\frac{1}{4}$ yd

Fabric B, $\frac{3}{8}$ yd

Fabric C, $\frac{5}{8}$ yd

Fabric D, $\frac{3}{8}$ yd

Fabric E, $\frac{1}{4}$ yd

Fabric F, $\frac{3}{8}$ yd

Fabric G, $\frac{1}{4}$ yd

$1\frac{1}{4}$ yd of white lining fabric, at least 39 in wide

Cardboard in two different colors for templates

Right-angled triangle

Steel ruler

Craft knife

Fabric-marking pen or pencil

Sewing equipment and threads

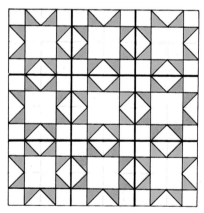

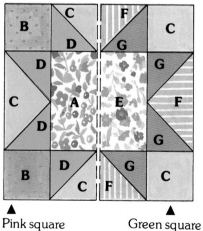

Pink square   Green square

Making the patchwork

1 Buy small amounts of your chosen fabrics, and plan your design. (You need not choose pink and green fabrics: any two constrasting groups of fabric could be used.) You must plan two different blocks. (The piecing diagram below shows half of each block.) Notice that one fabric, the light green (C), is used in both blocks; this helps to link the blocks visually and unify the design.

2 Label each fabric A, B, and so on, according to the position it occupies on the piecing diagram shown here. Then buy the specified amount of each fabric. Remember that you may need extra if you are positioning any patches by the window template method.

3 Using the craft knife and steel ruler, draw and cut the inner templates to the measurements shown below.

4 Using the first set of templates as a guide, draw and cut out a set of outer templates from constrasting cardboard, adding $\frac{3}{8}$ in seam allowance to each edge.

5 Using the larger set of templates, draw and cut out the pieces for the 5 green blocks: fabric A, 5 large squares; fabric B, 20 small squares; fabric C, 20 large triangles; fabric D, 40 small triangles.

6 Draw and cut the pieces for the 4 pink blocks: fabric E, 4 large squares; fabric C, 16 small squares; fabric F, 16 large triangles; fabric G, 32 small triangles.

7 Using the set of smaller templates, and working on the wrong side, draw the stitching lines for each patch. Keep the pieces for the pink blocks separate from those for the green blocks.

8 Join the pieces for each block, as shown in steps 6-8, page 55, first joining small pieces to make a strip and then joining the strips to make the block.

9 Similarly, join the completed blocks, following the piecing diagram for the cloth and joining 3 blocks to make a strip, then joining the three strips. Press the completed patchwork on the wrong side. It should measure approximately 37 in square.

Lining the patchwork

1 Lay the patchwork on the lining fabric and trim the lining to the same size.

2 Fold under $\frac{1}{2}$ in seam allowance on all four edges of both the patchwork and the lining and press. (The crease will serve as a guide when stitching.)

3 Place the patchwork and lining together with right sides facing. Pin and baste (optional) along the opened-out creases.

4 Starting in the middle of one side, stitch along the stitching line. End the stitching 10 in from the starting point. Press.

5 Turn the cloth right side out. Press. Slipstitch the opening edges together.

6 Topstitch all around the tablecloth about $\frac{1}{4}$ in from the edge.

Measurements for templates

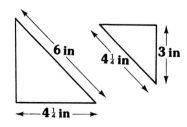

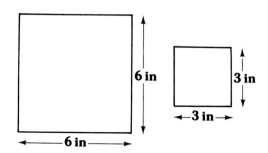

STREAK OF LIGHTNING QUILT

The effectiveness of this striking patchwork design depends on a careful choice of fabrics. The quilt shown uses several different black and white prints to contrast sharply with the solid red, gray, and white. If you are using a different color scheme, or wish to make a quilt (or other object) of a different size, first work out your own piecing diagram on graph paper (see "Designing," page 50). Number the rows as shown on page 65.

Size

approximately 60 in wide by 67½ in long

You will need:

1⅞ yd of red dressweight fabric, 36 in wide (includes fabric for binding)

1¼ yd each of white, gray, and black and white printed fabric, 36 in wide

3⅞ yd of dressweight fabric, any width, for lining

Piece of lightweight polyester batting 60 in by 67½ in

Cardboard for templates

Steel ruler

Right-angled triangle

Craft knife

Fabric-marking pencil or pen

Sewing equipment and threads

Making the patchwork

1 Using the craft knife and steel ruler, draw and cut 2 templates to the measurements shown on page 64. These are the cutting templates and include ⅜ in seam allowance. If you like, you can also cut templates for the finished size – 5 in by 2½ in and 2½ in square – and use these to mark the seamlines. However, this is not necessary for rectangular patches joined by machine, as it is relatively easy to stitch in a straight line.

2 Using the rectangular cutting template, mark and cut out 77 patches from the white fabric and 78 each from the red, gray, and black and white fabrics. Cut all the patches so that the long sides run along the crosswise grain.

3 Using the square cutting template, mark and cut out 8 patches from the white fabric and 6 each from the red, gray, and black and white fabrics. Pin these patches together in color groups with the pin running along the lengthwise grain. (This will help ensure that all the patches are joined on the same grain, so that the work will lie flat.)

4 Following the piecing diagram, join the patches to form horizontal rows: pin the patches together, right sides facing, and stitch ⅜ in from the edge. Press the seams to one side. Number each row as you complete it.

5 Pin and stitch the rows together. (You may prefer to join rows as you complete them, to prevent their getting mixed up.) Press. The completed patchwork should measure about 61 in wide by 68½ in long.

Quilting

1 Cut the lining fabric in half widthwise. Join the two halves lengthwise and press the seam open.

2 Lay the completed patchwork on top of the lining and trim the lining to the same size. Trim the batting, if necessary, to fit.

3 Place the three layers together on the floor, and pin them together over the entire surface at intervals of about 6 in. Then baste them together, working from the center outward as shown in steps 2 and 3, page 13.

4 Quilt along the seamlines, either by machine (see page 31) or by hand (see page 14).

5 From the remaining red fabric cut 8 strips, each 2½ in wide, on the crosswise grain. Join the strips to make one long strip, then cut this into 4 strips to fit the four sides of the quilt plus 1 in seam allowance. Turn under and press ½ in at each end of each binding strip.

6 Place one binding strip on a corresponding edge, with right side of binding to patchwork top and raw edges even. Pin, baste, and stitch the binding to the quilt, ½ in from the edge. Turn the binding back over the seam and press from the right side.

7 Fold the binding to the wrong side. Turn under ½ in along the raw edge and pin and baste the binding to the lining fabric. Hand-hem the folded edge in place.

8 Repeat steps 6 and 7 with the remaining strips. Slipstitch the folded edges at each corner.

Piecing diagram for quilt

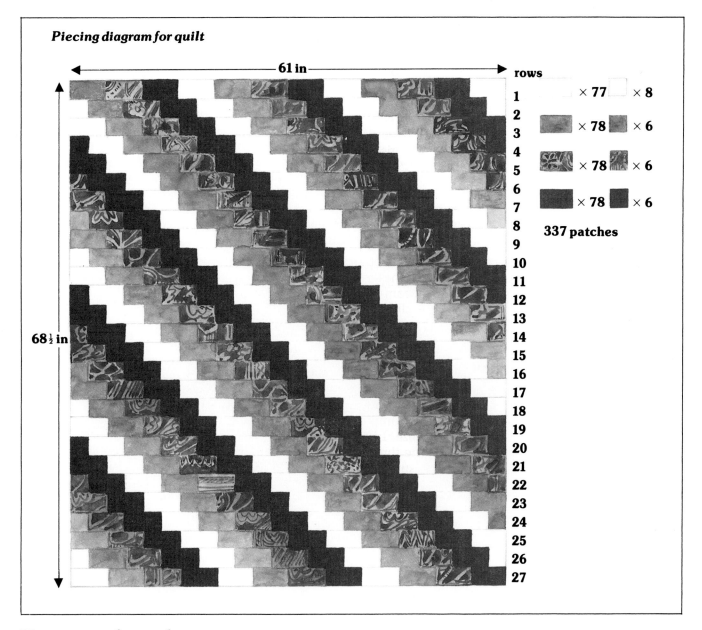

←————— 61 in —————→

rows

1
2
3
4
5
6
7
8
9
10
11
12
13
14
15
16
17
18
19
20
21
22
23
24
25
26
27

68½ in

×77   ×8

×78   ×6

×78   ×6

×78   ×6

337 patches

Measurements for templates

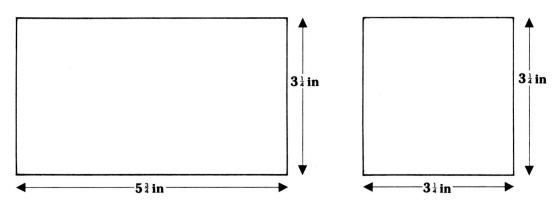

3¼ in

5¾ in

3¼ in

3¼ in

TRADITIONAL AMERICAN QUILTS

These two classic American designs make handsome quilts that will become family heirlooms. "Lady of the Lake," which originated in Vermont in the 19th century, is made by the usual block construction method. "Courthouse Steps" uses a variation of the log cabin method described on pages 91-95. Both are good designs for using up scraps of leftover fabric. However to give the designs unity it is important to repeat certain fabrics at key positions. The small red triangles and large red print triangles serve this purpose in the "Lady of the Lake" quilt.

"Lady of the Lake" quilt

1 Using graph paper (or plain paper and a right-angled triangle), draw 2 triangles to the measurements shown on page 68. (The measurements include $\frac{1}{4}$ in seam allowance.)

2 Glue the triangles to cardboard. Using the steel ruler and craft knife, cut out the templates.

3 Cut the required number of patches in each fabric, as follows: fabric A, 84 large triangles; fabric B, 84 large triangles and 1,008 small triangles; fabric C, 162 small triangles; fabric D, 846 small triangles.

4 Separate the patches for each of the 42 blocks that make up the quilt. For each block you will need: 2 large fabric A triangles, 2 large fabric B triangles, 4 small fabric C triangles, 24 small fabric B triangles, and 20 small fabric D triangles (2 of which – for the center of the block – should match).

5 Join the patches for each block as shown on the diagram. One quarter of the diagram has been labeled to show the arrangement of fabrics. Note that the D fabrics are placed at random in each block; but the center two triangles should match. First join the patches into strips (see the drawings below), and then join the strips to complete the block. Press the seam allowances to one side for additional strength.

6 When all the blocks are completed, arrange them in 7 rows of 6 blocks each, moving them around until you are satisfied with the effect. Note, however, that for the design to "read" correctly, large red triangles must be joined to large cream triangles. The small blue triangles at the corners produce a "windmill" motif when the blocks are joined.

7 Pin, baste (optional), and stitch the blocks into rows, then join the rows, taking $\frac{1}{4}$ in seam allowance.

8 Trim the batting, if necessary, to the same size as the patchwork.

9 Cut the lining fabric in half widthwise, then join the two halves lengthwise. Trim the fabric to measure $2\frac{1}{4}$ in larger, all around, than the patchwork.

10 Place the three layers together, with the lining on the bottom and the patchwork on top. Pin and then baste them together, working from the center to the sides and then to the corners.

11 Turn under and press $\frac{3}{8}$ in on the edges of the lining fabric. Bring the turned edges to the front, mitering the corners as shown on pages 166-167, and baste them in place, overlapping the patchwork by $\frac{1}{4}$ in. Slipstitch the hem in place.

12 Using the chenille needle and crochet cotton, tie the layers together at the corners and center point of each block (see page 29).

Size
approximately 79 in by $91\frac{1}{2}$ in

You will need:
Lightweight cotton fabrics, 36 in wide, in the following colors and amounts:

Fabric A (red print), $1\frac{1}{8}$ yd

Fabric B (cream-colored prints), total of $4\frac{5}{8}$ yd

Fabric C (blue print), $\frac{5}{8}$ yd

Fabric D (assorted prints in harmonizing shades of red, blue, yellow, and beige), total of 3 yd

$5\frac{1}{8}$ yd of 45 in-wide cotton fabric for lining and binding edges

Piece of polyester batting approximately 80 in by 92 in

Crochet cotton or other strong thread in color(s) matching the patchwork

Medium-sized chenille needle

Graph paper (optional)

Cardboard for templates

Steel ruler

Craft knife

Sewing equipment and threads

Joining triangles to form a strip

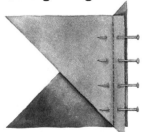

1 *Pin the triangles together so that their side edges cross at the seamline.*

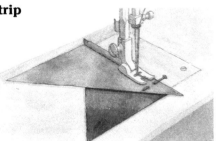

2 *Stitch the seam.*

3 *Press the seam allowances to one side. The long edges of the triangles are aligned.*

Piecing diagram (above) for "Lady of the Lake" block. The center 2 "D" triangles must match; elsewhere the various "D" fabrics may be used at random.

Measurements (below) for templates

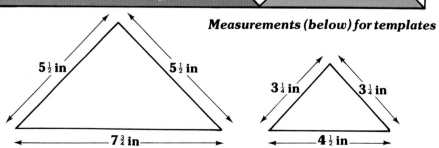

5 ½ in   5 ½ in

7 ¾ in

3 ¼ in   3 ¼ in

4 ½ in

Courthouse Steps quilt

1 Using graph paper, draw patterns for the templates: center square, $3\frac{1}{2}$ in by $3\frac{1}{2}$ in, 7 strips, each $1\frac{1}{4}$ in wide and the following lengths: $3\frac{1}{2}$ in, 5 in, $6\frac{1}{2}$ in, 8 in, $9\frac{1}{2}$ in, 11 in, $12\frac{1}{2}$ in. These measurements include $\frac{1}{4}$ in seam allowance. Cut out the patterns, glue them to the back of the fine sandpaper, and cut them out. (Make several of each template to allow for their becoming worn.)

2 Working on the wrong side of the fabric, draw and cut the patches for each block. Each round is made of 4 strips of the same fabric. Cut the center square of red fabric (or other solid color), then cut strips as follows: round 1, 2 of $3\frac{1}{2}$ in and 2 of 5 in; round 2, 2 of 5 in and 2 of $6\frac{1}{2}$ in; round 3, 2 of $6\frac{1}{2}$ in and 2 of 8 in; round 4, 2 of 8 in and 2 of $9\frac{1}{2}$ in; round 5, 2 of $9\frac{1}{2}$ in and 2 of 11 in; round 6, 2 of 11 in and 2 of $12\frac{1}{2}$ in. You will need strips for 40 blocks. Keep the strips for each block separate.

3 To join the patches, work as follows: first join the two $3\frac{1}{2}$ in strips to opposite sides of the center square. Press the seam allowances toward the strips. Join the remaining (5 in) strips of round 1 to the long sides of the previously-joined piece. You now have a piece 5 in square. Join the shorter strips of round 2 to the $3\frac{1}{2}$ in strips (and ends of 5 in strips) of round 1; join the longer strips of round 2 to the 5 in strips of round 1 and the ends of the strips just joined. Continue in this way, so that the longer strips of a round always overlap the ends of the shorter strips. Press all seam allowances away from the center. The completed block should measure $12\frac{1}{2}$ in square.

4 When all the blocks are completed, arrange 32 of them on the floor in the desired order, forming the rows shown in the diagram on page 70. The remaining 8 blocks will need to be cut into halves and quarters to fill in the sides. Use fabric-marking pen or tailor's chalk and, with the help of a ruler, draw a diagonal line between opposite corners. On one square draw another diagonal line, dividing it into quarters. Carefully cut along the marked lines of each block. Position the triangles along the edges of the quilt.

5 Starting at the upper right-hand corner, label the blocks and half blocks for each diagonal row – for example: A1, A2, A3. B1 ... B5, and so on.

6 Join the blocks and half blocks in each row, taking $\frac{1}{4}$ in seam allowance. On the last seam, end the stitching $\frac{3}{4}$ in from the side edge of the complete block where it meets the sharp angle of the triangle. (This is to allow for the necessary slight overlap of the block corner on the border strip when this is attached later.)

7 When all the rows have been joined, seam them to each other, matching corners carefully and again leaving $\frac{3}{4}$ in unstitched at the outer corners. Press the seams open.

8 Join the quarter blocks to the corners of the patchwork, again ending the stitching $\frac{3}{4}$ in from the raw edges of the complete blocks.

9 For the inner border cut 4 strips, each 4 in wide, of the border fabric, to fit the two short ends of the patchwork, plus 1 in, and 2 to fit the long sides, plus 7 in.

10 Pin, and baste one of the shorter strips to one short side of the patchwork, placing right sides together and taking $\frac{1}{4}$ in seam allowance on the patchwork and $\frac{1}{2}$ in on the border. Gently pull the corners of the complete blocks out of the way, so that the seam includes only the half and quarter blocks. Press the seam allowances toward the border. Attach the remaining shorter strip and then the two longer strips in the same way.

11 Trim the batting, if necessary, to measure the same as the quilt top.

Size

approximately 75 in by 93 in

You will need:

10 yd of assorted cotton or cotton-polyester fabrics, 45 in wide, for the patchwork strips

$\frac{1}{2}$ yd of 45 in cotton or cotton-polyester fabric in red (or other solid color) for the center squares

$1\frac{1}{2}$ yd of 45 in-wide cotton or cotton-polyester fabric for the inner border

$5\frac{5}{8}$ yd of 45 in-wide cotton or cotton-polyester fabric in a solid color for backing and binding

Piece of polyester batting at least 74 in by 92 in

Quilting thread to harmonize with patchwork

Graph paper

Fine sandpaper

Steel ruler

Craft knife or strong paper-cutting scissors

Fabric-marking pen

Sewing equipment and threads

12 Cut the lining fabric in half widthwise, then join the halves lengthwise. Press the seam open. Trim the lining to measure 1½ in more than the quilt top all around (that is, 3 in more in both directions). Press under ½ in on the long sides, then on the short sides.

13 Place the three layers together, centering the batting and the patchwork top over the wrong side of the lining. Pin and baste the layers together.

14 Quilt by hand (first placing the work in a hoop or frame, if you like), working outward from the center of each block toward the four corners. (If you prefer, you can simply tie the quilt at chosen points, as shown on page 29, using crochet cotton and a chenille needle.)

15 Fold one long side of the lining over to the front of the quilt, overlapping the edge by ½ in. Baste, then slipstitch the folded edge in place. Repeat on the opposite edge, then hem the short sides in the same way.

16 Slipstitch the gaps at the corners, then slipstitch the points of the outer blocks to the inner border.

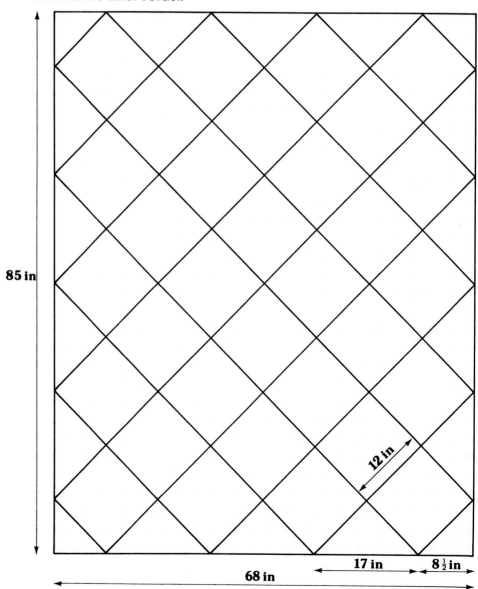

Piecing diagram for
"Courthouse Steps" quilt

FLOWERPOT QUILT

Patchwork and machine appliqué are combined in this handsome quilt, which will suit a double or queen-size bed. A subtle mixture of small-scale prints contrasts effectively with creamy white and beige. Before buying the specified amounts of your chosen fabrics, buy a small amount of each and arrange scraps of them on a piecing diagram of one section of the border (see "Designing" page 50). When you have decided on an arrangement, label each fabric A, B and so on, according to its position on the large piecing diagram on page 73.

Size

approximately 93 in wide by 100 in long

You will need:

6 different fabrics, each 48 in wide, in the following amounts:

Fabric A, 2⅜ yd

Fabric B, 1¾ yd

Fabric C, 2⅛ yd

Fabric D, 2½ yd

Fabric E, 1¼ yd

Fabric F, 1¼ yd

5⅝ yd of lining fabric, 48 in wide

Piece of lightweight polyester batting 100 in by 93 in

Cardboard for templates

Dressmaker's graph paper

Fabric-marking pencil or pen

Steel ruler

Craft knife

Sewing equipment and threads

Making the patchwork

1 Using dressmaker's graph paper, enlarge the flower motif as indicated on the pattern (see page 167). Cut out the individual parts of the enlarged pattern.

2 Also using the graph paper, draw and cut patterns for the three templates to the measurements shown on page 74. Glue them to the cardboard and, using the steel ruler and craft knife, cut out the cardboard templates. Make a few extra for each size, as they become worn after frequent use.

3 Cut the required number of patches in each fabric, as follows: fabric A, 12 squares, 36 large triangles, 204 small triangles, and the center square, 29 in by 36 in; fabric B, 108 small triangles; fabric C, 2 strips 64 in by 4 in, 2 strips 78 in by 4 in, and 78 small triangles; fabric D, 2 strips 43 in by 10 in, 2 strips 57 in by 4 in, 2 strips 86 in by 4 in, 2 strips 100 in by 4 in, and 30 small triangles; fabric E, 180 small triangles; fabric F, 96 small triangles.

Work on the wrong side of the fabric, placing the patches on the straight grain (indicated by the arrows on the template diagrams) and drawing around them with pencil or pen. Place them a generous ½ in apart, as shown. When cutting out, cut through the middle of this margin, thus adding ¼ in seam allowance to each patch. (A slightly more generous seam allowance has been included in the larger measurements to allow for error in cutting. Some of the strips may need to be pieced; allow extra for these seams.)

Pattern for appliqué motif

Each square = 1¼ in

Piecing diagram for quilt

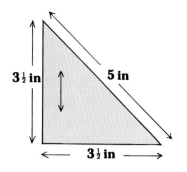

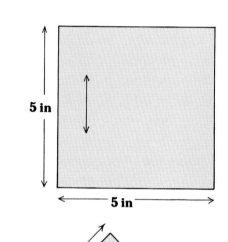

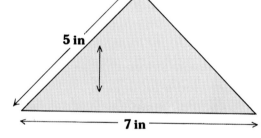

Measurements for templates

4 Cut the pieces for the appliqué from the remaining fabrics. Arrange these on the center square and pin and baste them in place. Press.

5 Set the machine to a wide, close zigzag stitch and stitch around the edges of each appliqué piece.

6 Following the piecing diagram, join the patches to make strips, pinning, basting (optional), and stitching along the marked seamlines. Press the seams as you go.

7 Starting from the center, with the appliquéd piece, join the patchwork strips, taking $\frac{1}{4}$ in seam allowance. (Check the fit of the center square; the allowance may be closer to $\frac{1}{2}$ in.) Press these seams open. Trim the ends of the plain fabric strips if necessary.

Quilting

1 Cut the lining fabric in half widthwise, and seam the two halves lengthwise. Press the seam open. Trim the lining to the same size as the top.

2 Trim the batting to the same size, if necessary.

3 Place the three layers together on a smooth, flat surface. Pin at intervals, then baste them together as shown in steps 2 and 3, page 13.

4 Place the work in a hoop or frame (see step 4, page 13), or simply lay it on a table, and quilt by hand, using a fine running stitch. First work around the edges of the appliqué design. Then work around each band of patches, as shown.

5 From the remaining piece of fabric B, cut 9 strips, $2\frac{1}{2}$ in wide. Join these to make one long binding strip, then cut the strip into 4 strips to fit the edges of the quilt, plus 2 in seam allowance. Press under 1 in at each end of each strip.

6 Place the strip along one corresponding edge of the patchwork, right sides facing and raw edges even. Pin, baste (optional) and stitch $\frac{1}{2}$ in from the edge. Press the seam, then fold the binding back over the seam and press from the right side.

7 Turn the binding to the wrong side. Fold under $\frac{1}{2}$ in along the raw edge and pin and baste this edge just over the stitching line. Hand-hem the binding in place.

8 Repeat with the remaining binding strips. Slipstitch the open ends at the corners.

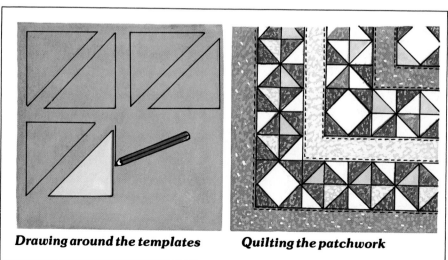

Drawing around the templates   **Quilting the patchwork**

BLOCK METHOD PATCHWORK
BABY'S EIDERDOWN COVER

A jolly circus tent, crowded with clowns, jugglers, a bareback rider, and an elephant, decorate this eiderdown cover. If you wish to make it for an eiderdown of a different size, adjust the design of the borders as necessary.

Size

approximately 39 in by 47 in

You will need:

Lightweight cotton or cotton-polyester fabrics, 36 in wide in the following colors and amounts:

White, ⅞ yd

Yellow, ⅝ yd

Red, ⅜ yd

Dark green, ⅜ yd

Scraps of dark blue, medium blue, dark red, light brown, medium brown, dark brown, light green, medium green, gray-green, black, orange and cream

1¾ yd of 45 in-wide dark blue cotton or cotton-polyester fabric for the bottom cover piece and patchwork background

1⅞ yd of white lawn for backing

Black stranded embroidery floss

Crewel needle, size 6

Tracing paper

Plain white paper or graph paper at least 10 in by 32 in

Cardboard for templates

Steel ruler

Craft knife

Sewing equipment and threads

Templates

1 To make the templates, first trace the shapes given on page 77. Add ¼ in seam allowance to the sides of each tracing. Glue each tracing to cardboard, then, using the steel ruler and craft knife, cut out each template. Number the templates 1 to 5 as shown. (You may wish to make several of each template to allow for their becoming worn with use.)

2 For the tent templates, enlarge the drawing given opposite as specified (see page 167). Trace each enlarged shape separately and add ¼ in seam allowance to all edges. Glue the tracings to cardboard and cut out the templates. Label them A to F as shown.

The central picture

1 For the clown, cut the required number of patches from each fabric, as follows: template 1, 19 of white, 3 of light brown, 3 of medium blue, 2 of dark red, 2 of yellow, 1 of orange, 1 of light green, 1 of medium green; template 2, 22 of white, 7 of medium green, 6 of red, 6 of light brown, 5 of light green, 5 of orange, 4 of yellow, 4 of medium blue, 3 of dark blue, 2 of dark red.

2 For the bareback rider, cut patches as follows: template 1, 31 of white, 5 of medium brown, 1 of yellow; template 2, 22 of white, 16 of medium brown, 6 of light brown, 4 of red, 3 of dark brown, 2 of yellow, 1 of black.

3 For the elephant, cut patches as follows: template 1, 27 of white, 23 of gray, 3 of medium blue; template 2, 9 of white, 7 of gray, 2 of medium blue, 2 of light brown, 1 of red, 1 of black.

4 For the jugglers, cut patches as follows: template 1, 28 of white, 5 of medium blue, 5 of red, 2 of light brown, 2 of light green, 2 of yellow; template 2, 19 of white, 4 of light brown, 3 of red, 3 of dark red, 3 of medium blue, 3 of light green, 3 of yellow, 2 of dark green.

5 Assemble the blocks for the four parts of the picture – clowns, bareback rider, elephant, and jugglers – using the method shown on page 55 and referring to the photograph on page 79.

6 Join the clown block to the bareback rider block, then the elephant to the jugglers. Finally, join the two pairs of blocks to make a piece of patchwork measuring approximately 25¾ in square. Press the seams open.

7 Cut the piece of white lawn to measure 40 in by 47½ in. Place the fabric on a flat surface with the shorter sides at top and bottom, and lay the patchwork right side up on top of it, with the upper edge of the patchwork 16¼ in from the upper edge of the lawn and the sides equidistant from the side edges of the lawn. Pin and baste it in place around the edges.

8 Stitch the two layers together by machine, working directly over the seam-

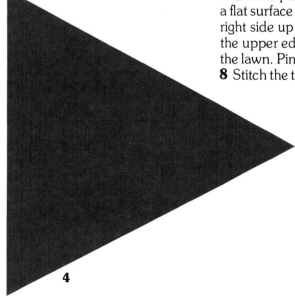

4

1

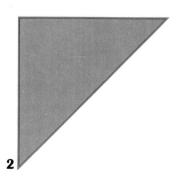

2

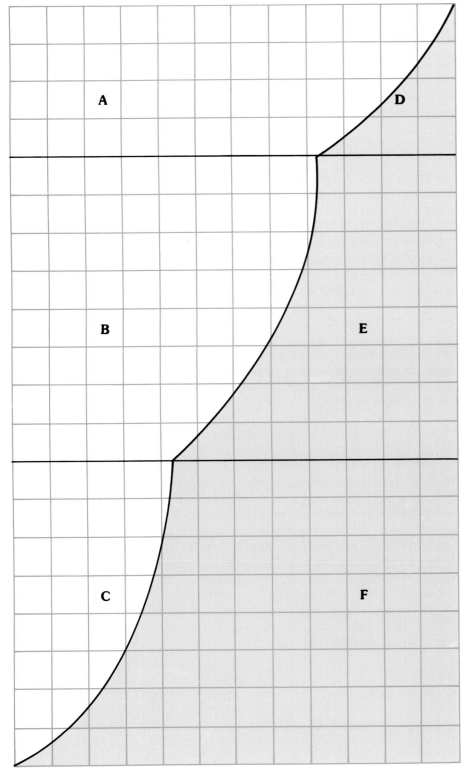

Each square = 1 in

A

B

C

D

E

F

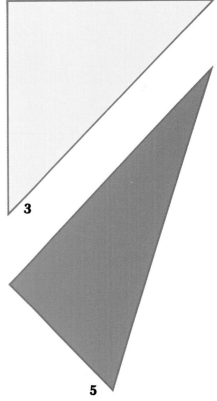

3

5

Pattern for tent templates (above)
Trace patterns for main templates (left and right)

lines between the four blocks so that the stitches are hidden in the seam.

9 Using 3 strands of embroidery floss in the crewel needle, embroider the eyes and mouth of each figure in the patchwork.

The borders

1 For the top inner border, cut the required number of patches from each fabric, as follows: template 3, 7 of white, 3 of yellow, 3 of red, 3 of medium green, 2 of light brown, 2 of dark red, 2 of orange, 2 of dark brown, 2 of dark blue, 1 of medium blue, 1 of gray-green, 1 of light green, 1 of dark green; template 2, 2 of white, 1 of yellow, 1 of medium blue.

2 For the bottom inner border, cut patches as follows: template 3, 6 of yellow, 4 of red, 3 of cream, 3 of medium blue, 3 of dark blue, 2 of dark green, 2 of medium green, 2 of light green, 2 of dark red, 2 of dark brown, 2 of orange, 1 of light brown.

3 Join the top inner border triangles as shown in the photograph to make 2 strips of triangles. Join the two strips to complete the border.

4 Place the border strip right side down on the patchwork, with raw edges even. Pin and baste it in place, then stitch, to join it to the central picture and the backing. Turn the strip right side up and press.

5 Following the arrangement shown in the photograph, join the triangles for the bottom inner border, first into squares and then into a strip.

6 Join the bottom border to the patchwork as described in step 4, above.

7 For the side borders, cut 8 strips, each $1\frac{1}{4}$ in by $32\frac{3}{8}$ in as follows: 4 of yellow, 2 of red, 2 of dark green. Stitch them together, taking $\frac{1}{4}$ in seam allowance, in this order: yellow, red, green. and yellow.

8 Attach the side borders to the patchwork as described in step 4, above, positioning the colors as shown in the photograph.

9 For the tent top, cut 2 strips of yellow, 1 of red, and 1 of green, each $1\frac{1}{4}$ in wide and 8 in long. Join them as for the side borders. Using template D, cut 2 patches (one with the template reversed), taking care that the colors will align with those in the side borders.

10 Cut 3 strips of red, 3 of dark green, and 2 of yellow, each $1\frac{1}{4}$ in by 16 in. Join them in this order: red, green, yellow, red, green, yellow, red, green. Using template E, cut 2 patches (one reversed) so that one patch has a red strip at its shorter side and the other has a green one.

11 Cut 5 strips of red, 5 of green, and 6 of yellow, each $1\frac{1}{4}$ in by $10\frac{1}{4}$ in. Join them to make 2 pieces: one in the order yellow, red, green, yellow, red, green, yellow, red, and the other in the order green, yellow, red, green, yellow, red, green, yellow. Using template F, cut 2 (mirror image) patches.

12 From the dark blue background fabric, cut 2 patches each (one reversed) of templates A, B, and C.

13 Stitch the corresponding patches of A and D, B and E, C and F together. (For a smooth curve, first draw the stitching line on the blue fabric.) Clip the curves and press the seam allowances toward the blue fabric.

14 Stitch the resulting 6 rectangles together to form the tent top.

15 Join the tent top to the inner border as described in step 4 above. Turn it right side up and baste it to the backing around the edges. Machine stitch along the curved outline of the tent, losing the stitches in the seam.

16 For the flag border cut the required number of patches from each fabric, as follows: template 4, 11 of blue background fabric, 6 of yellow, 6 of red, 5 of light brown, 5 of light green, 5 of dark red, 4 of medium green, 4 of cream, 3 of orange; template 5, 54 of dark blue background fabric.

17 Join the patches in the arrangement shown in the photograph to make the top border (23 large triangles) and side borders (13 large triangles each).
18 Join the top border and then the side borders as in step 4, above.
19 For the bottom (grass) border, cut patches as follows: template 2, 22 of light green, 10 of gray-green, 7 of dark green, 7 of medium green; template 3, 1 of light green.
20 Join the patches as shown in the photograph.
21 Join the bottom border as described in step 4, above.
22 To complete the top of the cover, cut 3 strips of dark blue background fabric, each 1¼ in wide, to fit the top and side edges. Cut another strip 2 in wide to fit the bottom edge. Pin and stitch the strips to the patchwork.

Completing the cover
1 Cut a piece of dark blue background fabric the same size as the top.
2 Place the patchwork top and the bottom piece together with right sides facing. Pin and stitch along the side and top edges, taking ¼ in seam allowance. Zigzag stitch the seam allowances together to finish them.
3 From medium green fabric cut 4 strips, each 1¼ in by 17 in. Fold each in half lengthwise and stitch along one end and down the side, ¼ in from the edges. Press the seam flat and turn the strip right side out. Press.
4 Turn up and press ¼ in along the lower edge of the cover. Turn up another ¾ in and press. Baste the hem in place. Pin the ties to the turned-up edge, 12 in from the corners. Hand-hem, securing the ties at the same time.

Ohio Star

Chevron

Nine-patch

Ribbons

MEDALLION PATCHWORK

A special kind of block method patchwork, medallion patterns were popular in England at the beginning of the 19th century. Quilts and coverlets were often made in these designs, which featured a large, eight-pointed star in the center, surrounded by several contrasting borders. Those made for special occasions often included a rich selection of the chintzes which were then becoming more readily available.

Although medallion patchwork is best kept square in shape, it can still be very versatile. A variety of patchwork patterns can be mixed together in one design, or a single block may be used fairly large in the center and then repeated on a smaller scale around the border. The designs lend themselves not only to quilts but also to tablecloths, wall hangings, and pillow covers — especially for large floor pillows.

Printed fabrics can be used effectively here, as in other patchwork. A print might make a useful contrast for a border, for example; or it could be used throughout the design. Small and larger-scale prints can be combined, as in the tablecloth shown on page 82.

It is best to start planning a medallion design from the center and work outward, keeping in mind the desired size of the finished work and its use. (If it is to be a pillow cover, for example, remember that the borders will curve away and so appear narrower.) For the center choose a symmetrical block pattern such as "Square Star" or "T Blocks" (see page 56). As this is the focal point of the design, it is best to keep the shapes comparatively large and simple, so that they catch the eye and at the same time contrast with the smaller pieces used in the surrounding borders. The center block may be set square or diagonally in relation to the rest of the design.

Borders are added to frame the center design. These can be of various widths, and may be simply a plain strip of fabric or a sequence of patchwork blocks. The measurement of each repeat in a border must divide exactly into the measurement of the center square: for example, if the square is 20 in on each side, the border repeat may be 2 in, or 4 in, or 5 in, but not 3 in or 6 in, since this would leave part of a repeat extending beyond the corners. The pattern may follow the same direction all the way around the border, or it may reverse direction in the center of each side to make a mirror image.

It is easiest to plan borders on graph paper along with the center design. The borders can be cut out and re-positioned until you achieve a pleasing combination. The corners may be an integral part of the border, so that the design flows smoothly around the center, or they may be treated as separate units, perhaps echoing the central image. A selection of popular border designs is given here.

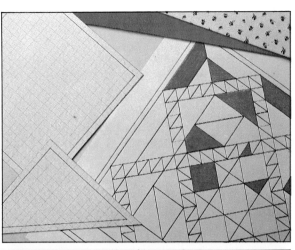

1 Designing Plan the entire design, small-scale, on graph paper. Tape a piece of tracing paper over the design and use this for planning the arrangement of the fabrics. Cut small squares of fabric and move them around over the design, trimming and combining them as necessary to fill the spaces. When you are satisfied with the effect, glue the pieces in place. Refer to this fabric design when cutting and joining the patches.

2 Making templates On the graph paper design, color in each different shape as a guide for making templates. Measure each shape and draw the corresponding template full size, keeping them in proportion. Add seam allowance to each template. It is useful to write on each template the number of patches required in each fabric.

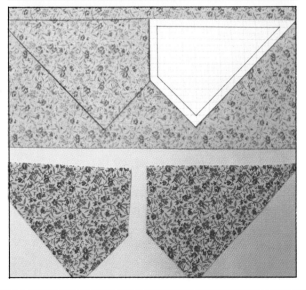

3 Mirror images Medallion patchwork often contains asymmetrical shapes which must be cut so that they form mirror images of each other. In this case, you should mark around the template in the usual way, then turn the template over to obtain the mirror image.

MEDALLION PATCHWORK TABLECLOTH

Use bright, contrasting fabrics for this tablecloth. First buy a small amount of your chosen fabrics and plan their placement. Label each fabric A, B, and so on, to correspond with its position on the piecing diagram on page 84.

Making the patchwork

1 Using the dressmaker's graph paper, enlarge the patterns for the 9 templates as indicated (see page 167). Add ⅜ in seam allowance to each pattern. Place the patterns on cardboard and mark and cut out the templates, using the steel ruler and craft knife.

2 Trim the seam allowance from each graph paper pattern. Glue the patterns to the contrasting cardboard, and cut around them to make the inner templates. Number the templates in both sets.

3 Using the outer templates and working on the wrong side of the fabric, cut the required number of patches from each fabric, as follows: template 1, 4 from fabric E, 8 from fabric D; template 2, 8 from fabric B; template 3, 8 from fabric E; template 4, 8 from fabric C (including 4 mirror images – see step 3, page 81); template 5, 4 from fabric A, 1 from fabric F; template 6, 4 from fabric A, 4 from fabric E, 8 from fabric B; template 7, 92 from fabric A, 64 from fabric B, 28 from fabric D; template 8, 4 from fabric B; template 9, 4 from fabric C, 4 from fabric D. To make identification easy, keep the patches together with their respective templates. This is especially important where shapes vary only slightly – as do templates 1 and 9, for example.

4 Using the set of smaller templates, and again working on the wrong side, draw the seamlines on each patch.

5 Join the patches to form each of the blocks and strips shown on the piecing diagram: pin, baste (optional), then stitch along the stitching lines. Press the seams as you go.

Size

approximately 55 in square

You will need:

6 different fabrics, each 36 in wide:

Fabric A, 1¾ yd	Fabric D, ⅝ yd
Fabric B, 2 yd	Fabric E, ⅝ yd
Fabric C, 1¼ yd	Fabric F, ¼ yd

3¼ yd of fabric for lining, any width (if 60 in fabric is used, only 1⅝ yd is required)

Crochet cotton in matching colors

Chenille needle, size 19 or 20

Dressmaker's graph paper

Cardboard in two different colors

Steel ruler

Craft knife

Fabric-marking pencil or pen

Sewing equipment and threads

Patterns for templates

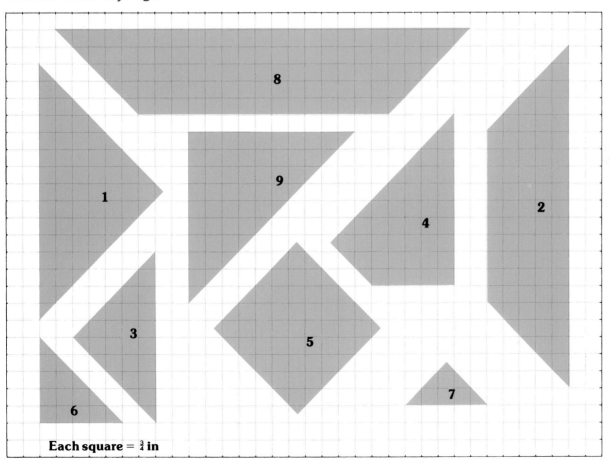

Each square = ¾ in

6 Join the blocks in the following order (see the diagram): join sections 1, 2, and 3, then join strips 4 and 5 to each side; join corners 6 and 7; add sections 8 and 9, then sections 10 and 11. Press all seams open.

7 From the remaining piece of fabric B, cut 7 strips on the crosswise grain, 2¾ in wide. Join these to make one long strip.

8 From the long strip cut 2 strips to fit 2 opposite sides of the patchwork. Seam them to the edges with right sides together and raw edges even, taking ⅜ in seam allowance. Press the seams open.

9 Cut 2 more strips to fit the remaining sides of the patchwork, including the first strips. Join them in the same way and press the seams open.

Finishing the tablecloth

1 Cut the lining fabric in half widthwise and seam the two halves lengthwise. Press the seam open. Trim the lining to measure the same as the patchwork.

2 Place the patchwork and lining together with right sides facing. Pin and baste them together around all four edges. Machine stitch around the edges, taking ⅜ in seam allowance and leaving a gap of about 12 in one side.

3 Turn the tablecloth right side out. Press the edges, rolling the seam slightly to the underside and tucking in the seam allowances on the opening. Baste the opening edges together.

13 Topstitch all around the patchwork, ⅛ in from the edge.

14 Using crochet cotton and the chenille needle, tie the patchwork to the lining at the points indicated by dots on the piecing diagram (see page 29).

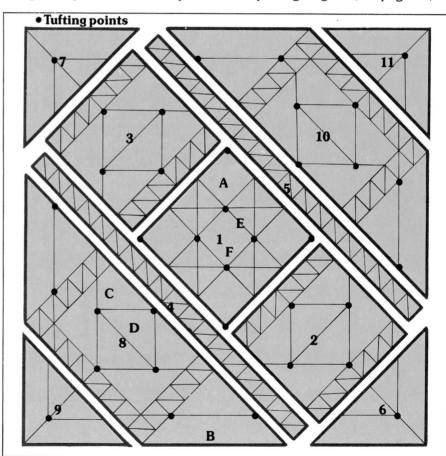

Piecing diagram for tablecloth

LATTICE STRIPS

Lattice strips are an effective way of setting patchwork blocks and can serve a variety of different functions: they can unify blocks pieced from different fabrics; they can frame a block that works better on its own than it does joined with identical blocks; and they can save time, cutting down the number of pieced blocks required to cover a given area.

The fabric used for the strips should be carefully chosen so that it will enhance the effectiveness of the blocks. In general, light-colored strips tend to open up a design and make it appear more spacious, whereas darker strips give a window-frame effect. Striped fabrics, cut with the stripes running along the length of the strips, can be used to accentuate the lattice pattern. Fabrics with an allover pattern usually make the strips less obvious, blending them with the rest of the patchwork. Because their purpose is to unify the design, they are best made from one fabric only, although a contrasting fabric may be used for the squares at intersections.

It is sometimes easiest to make the blocks first and choose the lattice fabric afterward. The completed blocks can be arranged on various fabrics or sheets of colored paper, with gaps left where the strips will be positioned. Play around with them until you have found the most attractive color combination.

It is best to cut lattice strips with the long edges running on the lengthwise grain. The strips and blocks can be set in a straight formation, or they can be set diagonally. In either case, it is best to join the strips with small blocks where they intersect – even where only one color is being used for the lattice; this helps to ensure that the main blocks will be aligned correctly.

1 Templates First plan the arrangement of blocks and lattice on graph paper. Then scale up (see page 167) the main block and the strip, making this the length of the block and the desired width, plus seam allowances. Use this pattern to cut the strip template. You will also need a template for the intersection squares measuring the same as the width of the strip. If the intersection square is to be patchwork, make the appropriate templates in the usual way.

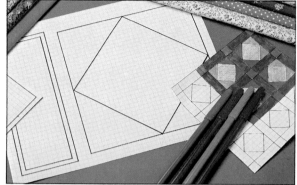

2 Diagonal designs If the lattice strips are to be set in on the diagonal, two additional, triangular, templates are needed: one half the size and the other a quarter the size of the finished intersection square, plus seam allowances. Extra templates will also be needed to make the half blocks around the edges of the design. (Do not simply cut a completed block in two, since the resulting half blocks would have no seam allowance along their diagonal edges.)

3 Joining a straight-set lattice Lay out all the patchwork sections as they are to be assembled. Join the units in rows, along one direction, joining strips and intersection squares, blocks and strips, as shown. When all the rows are joined, seam them to each other, being careful to check that the corners of the blocks exactly meet the corners of the small squares.

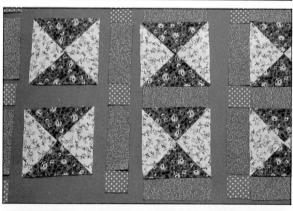

4 Joining a diagonal lattice Lay out the units as they are to be assembled. Start in the upper left corner with (in this example) a corner square. Then join the first row: half block, strip, half block. Row 2 will be half square, strip, square, strip, half square. Continue in this way, joining each completed row to the previous one, until the longest row is joined. Then start at the lower right corner and join rows as before. Finally, join the two sections of patchwork.

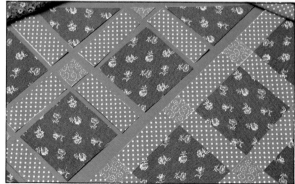

LATTICE STRIPS

"GOOSE IN THE POND" QUILT

Lattice strips are used to set off the traditional "Goose in the Pond" blocks of this quilt, which is finished by simply tying the layers together at intervals. Plan your colors carefully (see "Designing" page 50), using small amounts of fabric. Label the fabrics to correspond with their positions on the diagram on page 90. (Note that fabric E includes a selection of different light blue prints and that A is represented by two shades of dark blue simply to indicate joined pieces of the same fabric.)

Size

approximately 91 in by 112 in

You will need:

7 different fabrics, each 36 in wide, in the following amounts:

Fabric A, $4\frac{3}{8}$ yd

Fabric B, $2\frac{1}{4}$ yd

Fabric C, $3\frac{5}{8}$ yd

Fabric D, $2\frac{3}{4}$ yd

Fabric E, $2\frac{1}{2}$ yd (total)

Fabric F, $2\frac{3}{4}$ yd

$6\frac{3}{8}$ yd of fabric for lining, at least 48 in-wide

Piece of lightweight polyester batting, 91 in by 112 in

Crochet cotton, or other strong thread in colors to match the patchwork

Chenille needle, size 19 or 20

Graph paper

Tracing paper

Cardboard for templates

Steel ruler

Craft knife

Sewing equipment and threads

Making the patchwork

1 Using graph paper, draw template patterns for templates 1, 2, and 3, to the measurements shown on page 89. Trace template 5. Use the tracing paper and a ruler to draw patterns for templates 4, 6, 7, and 8, which are subdivisions of template 5. Add $\frac{1}{4}$ in seam allowance to each pattern and cut it out.

2 Glue each pattern to cardboard and cut out the template, using the steel ruler and craft knife. (Make some extra templates to allow for their becoming worn.)

3 Working on the wrong side of the fabric, draw and cut out the required number of patches for each template as follows: template 1, 31 from fabric F; template 2, 32 from fabric B, 32 from fabric D, 64 from fabric C, 128 from fabric A, 232 from fabric E; template 3, 336 from fabric A, 420 from fabric C; template 4, 144 from fabric B, 144 from fabric C; template 5, 64 from fabric C; template 6, 360 from fabric D; template 7, 88 from fabric E; template 8, 84 from fabric D, 88 from fabric A. Keep all the patches with their respective templates.

4 Following the diagram on page 90, join the appropriate patches to make one block (the area inside the lattice strips). Pin, baste (optional), and machine stitch the pieces together to form strips, taking $\frac{1}{4}$ in seam allowance. Press the seams as you go. Then join the strips to complete the block. Make 11 more blocks in the same way.

5 Make the patchwork intersection squares (formed from 9 squares cut from template 3). Make a total of 36, then set 16 of these aside to be used later for the quilt corners.

6 Join the lattice strips, intersecting squares, and blocks to make horizontal rows, following the diagram. (Note that this shows one-quarter of the quilt, which includes 3 blocks across its width and 4 along its length.) Press the seams flat. Then join the rows to make the center section. Press. The work should now measure approximately 68 in by 89 in.

7 Make the inner border for each side of the quilt, using patches cut from template 2. For the shorter borders use 50 patches of fabric E and 7 of B, as shown on the diagram. For the longer borders use 60 of fabric E and 9 of B. Press the seams flat.

8 Make the middle border for each side, using squares cut from template 7 (fabric E) surrounded by 4 triangles cut from template 6 (fabric D). The shorter borders contain 19 complete squares; the longer borders contain 25. Press the seams flat.

9 Make the outer border for each side, beginning with the strip of triangles. For this, make rectangles from 1 triangle cut from template 8 (fabric A) and 2 from template 6 (fabric D). Join 19 rectangles to make strips for the shorter sides; join 25 to make the strips for the longer sides. Press the seams flat.

10 From fabric A, cut and piece enough $2\frac{1}{4}$ in-wide strips to fit each of the four borders. Join each strip to one of the patchwork strips constructed in step 8. Press the seams flat.

11 Make the corner blocks of the quilt, which are identical to the center sections of the "Goose in the Pond" blocks.

12 Join the three border sections together, following the diagram. Join a corner block to each end of both shorter borders.

13 Join the longer borders to the main patchwork section. Then join the remaining borders to the top and bottom edges of the patchwork.

14 From fabric A, cut and piece enough $2\frac{3}{8}$ in-wide strips to fit each of the four sides of the quilt. Join the side strips, then the top and bottom strips, to the four edges. Press.

Quilting

1 Cut the lining fabric in half widthwise. Seam the two halves lengthwise and press the seam open. Trim the lining so that it measure $\frac{3}{4}$ in less than the patchwork on all sides.

2 Trim the batting, if necessary, to the same size as the lining fabric.

3 Place the patchwork, right side down, on the floor. Lay the batting on top of it, then lay the lining fabric, right side up, on top. Make sure that the patchwork extends $\frac{3}{4}$ in on each side. Pin and baste the three layers together, from the center outward (see steps 2 and 3, page 13).

4 Fold the edge of the patchwork over the batting and lining. Turn under about $\frac{1}{4}$ in on the raw edge and pin and baste it to the lining fabric. Hand-hem the folded edge in place, mitering the corners (see page 166). Press.

5 Using the crochet cotton and chenille needle, tie the layers together (see page 29) at each corner of every block.

Templates 1, 2, and 3

$3\frac{1}{2}$ in | $3\frac{1}{2}$ in | $1\frac{1}{8}$ in | $1\frac{1}{8}$ in

$17\frac{3}{4}$ in | $1\frac{1}{8}$ in

Templates 4, 5, 6, 7, and 8

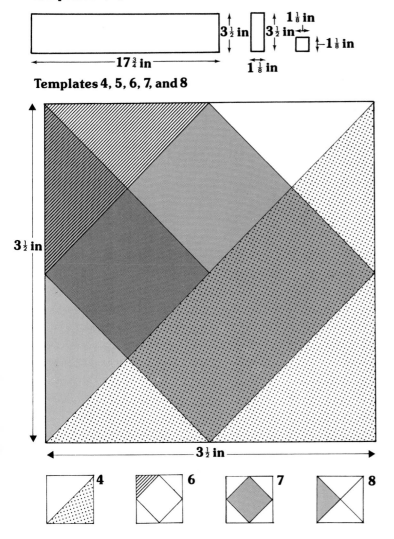

$3\frac{1}{2}$ in

$3\frac{1}{2}$ in

4   6   7   8

Measurements and trace patterns for templates

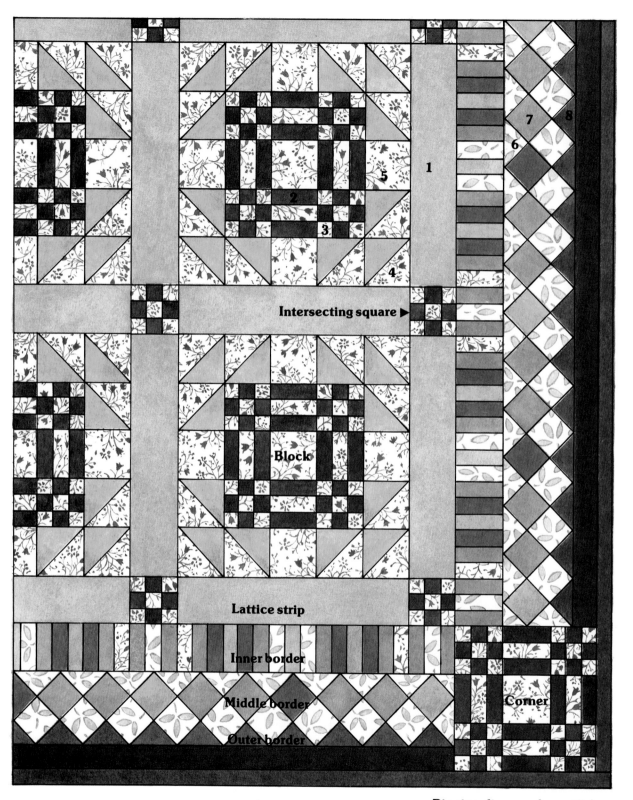

Legend:
A
B
C
D
E
F

1
2
3
4
5
6
7
8

Intersecting square ▶

Block

Lattice strip

Inner border

Middle border

Outer border

Corner

C = center point of quilt

Piecing diagram for quilt (one quarter)
Numbers refer to templates.

LOG CABIN PATCHWORK

Although basically a block-method type of patchwork, log cabin is quite distinct from other block designs, both visually and in the details of its construction. It is formed from narrow strips of fabric surrounding a central square in a contrasting fabric. The arrangement of the strips is said to represent the overlapping of logs in the walls of the log cabins built by early American settlers. According to tradition, the central square represents the fire in the hearth (and, for this reason, was usually red); the light-colored strips on one side of the block suggest the light within the cabin, and the dark strips the shadows.

By arranging the completed blocks in various ways it is possible to create strikingly different patterns of light and shade — some of which are shown here and on page 92. And although the light-dark contrast is usually achieved diagonally within the block, it can, instead, be produced horizontally and vertically, by placing the dark strips and light strips on opposite sides, as shown in the "Courthouse Steps" variation on page 57. Here, the "step" effect is produced mainly by overlapping all the strips on two opposite sides, rather than by overlapping ends in a clockwise sequence, as in

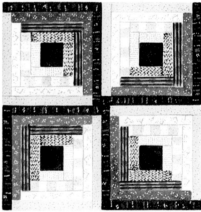

Windmill Blades: in this pattern, light and dark alternate around a central point.

Straight Furrow: this pattern is marked by strong diagonal lines.

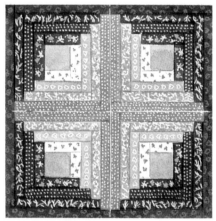

Light and Dark: a cross emerges if the light strips are grouped together.

Courthouse Steps: here, light and dark are on opposite sides, and the strips overlap symmetrically.

most log cabin patchwork. An effect of concentric frames can be created by abandoning the light-and-shadow arrangement of colors and using the same color for each round. An example of this approach is the "Courthouse Steps" quilt on page 66.

There are two basic ways of constructing log cabin blocks. One way is simply to stitch the strips together as for ordinary patchwork. Another way is to stitch the strips to a piece of backing fabric, interfacing, or batting, cut to the size of the finished block plus seam allowances. This "quilt-as-you-go" method is the preferred one for fabrics that are slippery. Although the completed block is thicker than if the first method were used, the use of a lightweight backing fabric will keep bulk to a minimum; and in some cases – such as a bedspread or quilt – the extra weight may be desirable. The use of batting eliminates the need for any further padding: only a lining is required. The method shown on pages 94-95 includes squares of lining, so that the blocks, once joined, need no further finishing.

Fabrics The usual criteria for patchwork fabrics apply here, too: the fabric should take a crease well and should not be too stretchy. Medium-weight fabrics are generally suitable. If the object is intended to be hard-wearing (such as the rug shown on page 96), a furnishing-weight cotton may be the best choice. If you are using the "quilt-as-you-go" method, you can mix fabrics a bit more freely, since they are attached to a firm foundation fabric or to batting.

Both prints and solid colors may be used, although prints should be small-scale, and it is customary to use a solid color for the central "fire." If you wish to create a light-dark pattern, you must buy equal amounts of fabric in the two contrasting color ranges. It is not necessary to use extremes of light and dark: the gradual shading of warm tones in the rug on page 96 is quite effective.

Buy a small amount of a variety of fabrics in the two color ranges and experiment with them (see "Designing," page 50), then calculate the amount required of each as explained on page 51.

If you are using the "quilt-as-you-go" method, you will also need backing fabric. This could be lightweight interfacing, unbleached muslin, or thin batting, depending on the desired effect.

Measuring and marking equipment Templates are not absolutely necessary for log cabin patchwork: you can mark the strips on the fabric as for Seminole patchwork (see page 137) if you like. However, if the fabrics are at all slippery, you will find it easier to use templates. Make them from fine sandpaper (first making graph paper patterns if you prefer).

BASIC METHOD

1 Planning the design Make a rough, colored plan of the item you would like to make, showing the pattern of light and shade across the blocks. Then make a full-size plan of one block on graph paper. The strips must all be the same width, but the central square can be larger. Arrange sample strips of fabric on the design until you are pleased with the effect. Label the fabrics and mark these numbers or letters on the diagram.

2 Cutting templates and strips Measure each strip on your diagram and add $\frac{1}{4}$ in all around for seam allowances. On the back of fine sandpaper mark the dimensions of each unseamed strip. Cut out the templates, using a ruler and craft knife. (You will have some duplicates, but you will need them as the first become worn.) With the fabric wrong side up, mark around the templates (the sandpaper prevents the fabric from slipping). Cut out the strips.

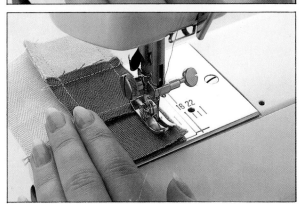

3 Joining strips Place the shortest strip along one side of the central square, with right sides facing, and stitch $\frac{1}{4}$ in from the edges. Press the seam toward the strip. Stitch this joined piece to the next strip (working in a clockwise direction, viewed from the right side).

4 Continue joining strips, working around the central square and always pressing the seam allowances away from the central square. In this picture, the second dark-colored strip (underneath) is being joined to the first strip, the square, and the third (dark) strip.

"QUILT-AS-YOU-GO" METHOD

1 Cutting out Cut the center square and the lining square (if used) to the finished size plus seam allowances. Cut the batting the exact finished size. (For accuracy, it is advisable to make templates for these three shapes.) Cut the required fabric strips (see step 1 of Basic method), including seam allowances on all edges. If you are sewing by hand, mark the stitching lines on the wrong side of the fabric. Using a fabric-marking pen, draw 2 diagonal lines on the batting to serve as guides for positioning.

2 Stitching Pin the center square to the batting, then pin the first (shortest) strip along one edge, right sides facing. Stitch it in place by machine or by hand, using a small running stitch. If you are including the lining in the work, finish the thread ends neatly by bringing them to the right side and tying them (they will be hidden under the next strip); trim the ends. Do not use reverse stitching. Fold the strip over to the right side and pin it to the batting.

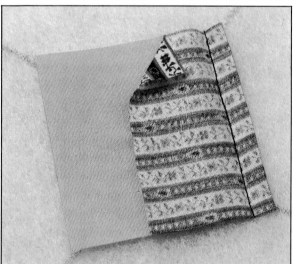

3 Continue joining strips in the same way, working in a clockwise direction around the center square and adding 2 light and 2 dark strips alternately (unless a different pattern is desired). The completed block should be the finished size plus seam allowances; in this example the patchwork measures the same as the lining piece.

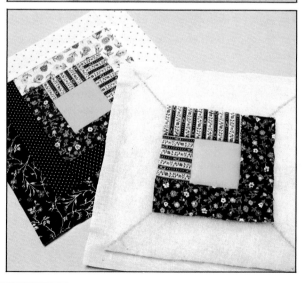

4 Joining blocks First cut a strip of lining fabric 1 in wide and the length of one side of the block. Pin 2 blocks together with right sides facing and the strip right side down on the uppermost block. Baste and stitch through all five thicknesses, taking $\frac{1}{4}$ in seam allowance. Place the blocks flat, lining side up. Turn the binding over as shown, turn under $\frac{1}{4}$ in on its raw edge, and sew it to the lining, covering the seam.

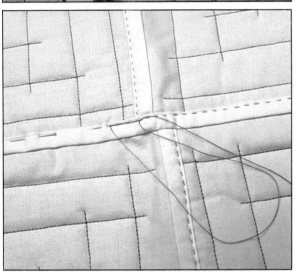

5 Assembling the blocks Join the blocks in rows, as described in step 4, making sure that the pattern is formed correctly on the patchwork side. Then join the rows, using the same method as for the individual blocks, and a strip cut to the correct length. Make sure that the crossing seams are aligned correctly.

6 Quilting with a separate lining The method shown in steps 1-5 can be adapted in various ways: the batting can be eliminated and the patchwork sewn instead to a piece of unbleached muslin or interfacing; or the batting can be used without a lining underneath. In either case, a separate lining will usually be needed. This is joined to the edges of the patchwork and then further secured either by tying (see page 29) or by hand-quilting, as shown here.

LOG CABIN RUG

Warm shades of gold and rust are used for this log cabin patchwork rug. Sturdy furnishing-weight fabrics and a layer of batting give it the necessary thickness: if you prefer, you could machine-quilt each block separately (see page 94). Using the same basic design, you could make an attractive wall hanging, perhaps using lighter-weight fabrics in contrasting prints and substituting interfacing for the batting.

Making the patchwork

1 Using the sandpaper, mark and cut the following templates: center square (and first strip) $1\frac{3}{4}$ in by $1\frac{3}{4}$ in and 8 strips, each $1\frac{3}{4}$ in wide and the following lengths: 3 in, $4\frac{1}{4}$ in, $5\frac{1}{2}$ in, $6\frac{3}{4}$ in, 8 in, $9\frac{1}{4}$ in, $10\frac{1}{2}$ in, $11\frac{3}{4}$ in. All of the templates include $\frac{1}{4}$ in seam allowance. To ensure that all angles are exactly 90°, either draw the shapes on graph paper, then glue these patterns to the back of the sandpaper, or check each angle with a triangle. Use a steel ruler and craft knife to cut out the templates.

2 Using the templates, cut the required pieces for each block, placing the templates on the wrong side of the fabric and drawing around them carefully with the pen or pencil. Take care to align the templates with the straight grain of the fabric. Note that for each block you will need to cut 2 pieces of each size template, except for the largest. The smallest template is used for the center square (fabric F) and one piece of the lighter fabric; the largest is used for one strip of the darker fabric. Use the remaining templates to cut one light and one dark strip. Keep all the pieces for each block together.

3 Begin the patchwork by making the block using fabrics A and B. Join the fabric A square (the first strip) to the center square as shown in step 3, page 93, taking $\frac{1}{4}$ in seam allowance. Press the seam allowances away from the center square.

4 Join the 3 in fabric A strip to the first two pieces. (See the piecing diagram for the block, below.) Pin the pieces together, then turn them right side up to double check that the fabric A strips lie below and to the left of the center square.

5 Next, join the 3 in fabric B strip to the end of the end of the last strip and the center square. Continue adding strips in this way, working clockwise (viewing the work from the right side), and pressing seams outward as you go, until the last strip has been joined. The completed block should measure $11\frac{3}{4}$ in square.

6 Make the remaining 5 blocks in the same way, taking care to follow the same joining sequence, so that the strips will overlap in the same way on all the blocks.

7 Pin, baste (optional), and stitch 3 blocks together to make one row, taking $\frac{1}{4}$ in seam allowance, and referring to the plan of the rug at right. Join the other three blocks, then join the two rows to complete the patchwork.

Finishing the rug

1 From the remaining piece of fabric F, cut a piece to measure $\frac{3}{4}$ in larger all around than the patchwork; this will be the lining. Also cut 4 strips, each $3\frac{1}{4}$ in wide and the length of the patchwork edges, plus $\frac{3}{8}$ in seam allowance. Turn under and press $\frac{3}{8}$ in at each end of each binding strip.

2 Lay the lining right side down on a flat surface. Place the batting and the patchwork, right side up, on top. Make sure that the patchwork is centered. Pin, then baste the three layers together, from the center outward.

3 Place one short binding strip on a short end of the patchwork, with right sides together, and raw edges even. Pin, baste, and machine stitch, $\frac{1}{4}$ in from the edge. Turn the binding right side up, over the seam; press.

4 Turn the binding to the underside of the rug. Fold under $\frac{1}{4}$ in on the raw edge of the binding, and pin, baste, and hand-hem it over the stitching line on the underside. Press.

5 Repeat steps 3 and 4 to bind the other short side and the long sides of the rug. Slipstitch the ends of the binding at each corner.

6 Spray the underside of the rug with liquid latex, if desired, to prevent it from slipping.

The piecing diagram for a single block (right), showing the sequence of joining, seen from the wrong side, and (above) the diagram for the rug

Size
25 in by 36 in

You will need:
6 different furnishing-weight cotton fabrics, each 48 in wide, in the following amounts:

Fabric A, $\frac{1}{8}$ yd

Fabric B, $\frac{3}{8}$ yd

Fabric C, $\frac{3}{8}$ yd

Fabric D, $\frac{1}{4}$ yd

Fabric E, $\frac{1}{8}$ yd

Fabric F, $\frac{7}{8}$ yd

Piece of lightweight polyester batting, 24 in by $35\frac{1}{2}$ in

Sandpaper for templates

Graph paper or right-angled triangle

Fabric-making pencil or pen

Steel ruler

Craft knife

Liquid latex spray (optional)

Sewing equipment and threads

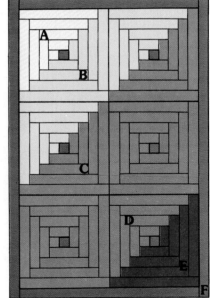

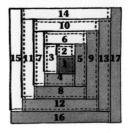

OCCASIONAL TABLE COVER

This elegant patchwork table cover is made from paisley-printed silk fabrics in shades of red and blue. Sixteen blocks measuring 8¾ in square, make up the cover.

Making the patchwork

1 Using fine sandpaper, cut the following templates (first making graph paper patterns if you like): center square $1\frac{3}{4}$ in by $1\frac{3}{4}$ in; 13 strips, each $1\frac{1}{8}$ in wide and the following lengths: $1\frac{3}{4}$ in, $2\frac{3}{8}$ in, 3 in, $3\frac{5}{8}$ in, $4\frac{1}{4}$ in, $4\frac{7}{8}$ in, $5\frac{1}{2}$ in, $6\frac{1}{8}$ in, $6\frac{3}{4}$ in, $7\frac{3}{8}$ in, 8 in, $8\frac{5}{8}$ in, $9\frac{1}{4}$ in. All of the templates include $\frac{1}{4}$ in seam allowance on each edge.

2 Using the templates, cut the required pieces for each block. Cut the center square once in bright-colored fabric; cut the shortest strip once in another bright-colored fabric. Cut the next size strip in the same bright-colored fabric and in a dark-colored fabric. Continue in this way, cutting each template (except the last one) in both bright and dark-colored fabric and making sure that the same bright or dark fabric is used for neighboring strips on the same level. Cut the longest template once from the appropriate dark-colored fabric. Keep all the pieces for each block together.

3 Join the strips as shown in steps 3 and 4, page 93, taking $\frac{1}{4}$ in seam allowance. Press the seam allowances outward as you go.

4 Join 4 squares to make one-quarter of the cloth, placing the darker sides of the squares together as shown in the diagram. Press the seams open. Join the remaining groups of squares in the same way.

5 Join the four quarters to complete the patchwork. It should measure $35\frac{1}{2}$ in square. Press.

Size
approximately 39 in square

You will need:

6 different dark-colored printed fabrics (e.g. dark blue), 36 in-wide: $\frac{1}{8}$ yd of each for the inner strips and $\frac{1}{4}$ yd of each for the outer strips

6 different bright-colored printed fabrics (e.g. red), 36 in-wide: $\frac{1}{8}$ yd of each for the inner strips and $\frac{1}{4}$ yd of each for the outer strips

$\frac{1}{8}$ yd of bright-colored printed fabric, 36 in-wide, for the center squares

$\frac{3}{8}$ yd of 45 in-wide fabric (printed or solid-color) for the border

$1\frac{1}{4}$ yd of 45 in-wide fabric for lining

Fine sandpaper for templates

Graph paper (optional)

Steel ruler

Craft knife

Sewing equipment and threads

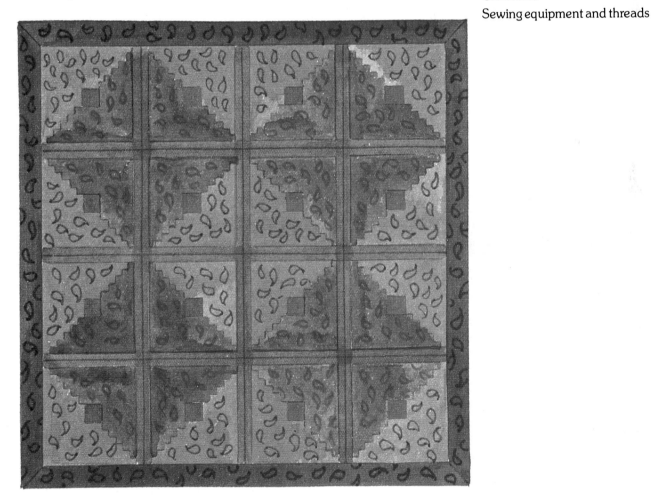

Finishing the tablecover

1 Trim the lining fabric to measure $2\frac{1}{2}$ in more than the patchwork all around. (It is most important that this measurement be exact.) Pin and baste the patchwork to the lining, wrong sides facing, centering it carefully.

2 From the border fabric cut 4 strips, each $3\frac{1}{4}$ in by the width of the backing.

3 Pin each border strip to one edge of the lining fabric, with the right side of the strip to the underside (i.e. right side) of the lining. Where the strips meet at the corners, fold each back on itself, forming a 45° angle. Press.

4 Unpin the strips within a few inches of each corner. Pin the corners of the strip together along the diagonal creases and stitch, following the crease lines carefully and stopping a little over $\frac{1}{2}$ in from the end. Trim the seam and press it open.

5 Baste the border to the lining and machine stitch around all four edges, taking $\frac{5}{8}$ in seam allowance. Press the seam flat.

6 Turn the border over to the top of the cover. Press the seamed edge. Turn under $\frac{3}{8}$ in along the raw edges of the border, and pin and baste the folded edge to the patchwork, overlapping its raw edges by $\frac{1}{4}$ in. (If necessary, adjust the margin on the border to ensure that the finished width of the outer patchwork strip is exactly $\frac{5}{8}$ in; slight irregularities in the width of the border will be less apparent.) Slipstitch the border in place; press.

Mitering a border

1 Pin the border strips to the lining (wrong side of border to right side of lining). Fold the corners back as shown.

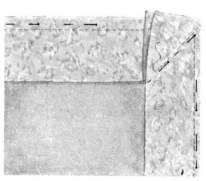

2 Stitch the corners together along the fold lines, stopping $\frac{1}{2}$ in from the inner edges. Trim the seam and press it open.

3 Stitch the border in place around the edges. Bring it to the right side; turn under the edges and slipstitch them in place.

QUILTED DECKCHAIR COVER

A piece of quilted log cabin patchwork makes a handsome cover for an ordinary deckchair. The blocks are pieced using the "quilt-as-you-go" method and backed with a single piece of fabric. Strips of nylon tape attach the cover to the canvas sling.

Size

approximately 19 in by 50 in
(The unseamed patchwork blocks
measure 8 in square, but a certain
amount of shrinkage occurs during
joining. The size of the finished cover
can be adjusted by making the
border strips wider or narrower.)

You will need:

$\frac{1}{2}$ yd each of 6 different printed
fabrics, each 36 in wide (fabrics
A,B,C,D,E and F – the first 3
light-toned, the second 3
dark-toned)

$2\frac{1}{4}$ yd of 36 in-wide solid-colored
fabric for lining, border, and center
squares

1 yd of 45 in-wide lightweight
polyester batting

$1\frac{1}{4}$ yd of 1 in-wide bias binding or
ribbon

Heavy crochet cotton and chenille
needle, size 19 or 20; or quilting
thread

1 yd of nylon fastening tape

Cardboard

Right-angled triangle

Ruler

Craft knife

Fabric marking pen

Sewing equipment and threads

Making the patchwork

1 Using the cardboard, mark and cut the two square templates: one measuring $2\frac{1}{2}$ in for the center square, and one measuring 11 in for the batting. For this project the batting is cut larger than the finished block, instead of smaller, to accommodate the border strips, which are attached later.

2 Use the smaller template to cut 12 squares from the solid-colored fabric, and use the larger template to cut 12 squares of batting.

3 Mark each batting square with 2 diagonal lines from corner to corner, and pin a fabric square to the center, as shown in step 1, page 94.

4 From the printed fabrics, cut $1\frac{1}{2}$ in-wide strips on the lengthwise grain: 6 strips each of fabrics A and D and 12 strips of each of fabrics B, C, E, and F. If you are sewing the patchwork by hand, mark the stitching lines, $\frac{1}{4}$ in from each long edge.

5 For each block, cut the following short strips from the long ones already cut: fabric A, 1 strip $2\frac{1}{2}$ in and 1 strip $3\frac{1}{2}$ in; fabric D, 1 strip $3\frac{1}{2}$ in and 1 strip $4\frac{1}{2}$ in; fabric B, 1 strip $4\frac{1}{2}$ in and 1 strip $5\frac{1}{2}$ in; fabric E, 1 strip $5\frac{1}{2}$ in and 1 strip $6\frac{1}{2}$ in; fabric C, 1 strip $6\frac{1}{2}$ in and 1 strip $7\frac{1}{2}$ in; fabric F, 1 strip $7\frac{1}{2}$ in and 1 strip $8\frac{1}{2}$ in.

6 Pin the shorter strip of fabric A to one side of the center square, right sides facing, baste (optional), and stitch, as shown in step 2, page 94, taking $\frac{1}{4}$ in seam allowance. Turn the strip to the right side and pin it in place. (There is no need to finish the thread ends neatly, since the stitching will be hidden by the lining.)

7 Join the remaining strips in the same way, applying them in the order given in step 5 above and working in a clockwise direction around the center square. When all the strips have been joined, baste around the outer strips, $\frac{5}{8}$ in from the edge.

8 When all the blocks have been made, arrange them as shown in the photograph on page 103. Number the blocks 1 to 12 with bits of paper, also indicating the top edge, to ensure that you join then correctly.

9 From the solid-colored fabric, cut 12 strips, each 3 in wide and the length of one side of the patchwork (which should be $8\frac{1}{2}$ in).

10 Place a strip on the outside edge of each patchwork block, right sides facing and fabric edges matching. Pin, baste (optional), and stitch each strip in place, working through all three layers and taking $\frac{1}{4}$ in seam allowance. Turn the strips right side up and baste them to the batting.

11 Trim the batting to measure a scant $\frac{3}{8}$ in less than the patchwork on all four sides of blocks 3 – 10. On blocks 1, 2, 11 and 12, trim the batting as for the other blocks except for the top edges of 1 and 2 and the bottom edges of 11 and 12.

12 Join the blocks in horizontal pairs, taking $\frac{1}{4}$ in seam allowance; then join the pairs to complete the patchwork.

13 Cut 2 more strips of the solid-colored fabric, 3 in by 21 in (to fit the top and bottom edges). Attach these to the remaining edges of the patchwork as described in step 10, above. Trim the batting as in step 11.

Assembling the cover

1 From the solid-colored fabric cut a piece for the lining the same size as the finished patchwork. Also cut 2 pieces for the flaps used to attach the cover: each 4 in by 20 in.

2 Turn under and press $\frac{1}{4}$ in on the short ends of each flap, then turn under another $\frac{1}{4}$ in and topstitch. Repeat on one long side of each flap.

3 Place each flap right side down on one end of the patchwork, with the raw edges of the flap and the border strip even. The side edges of the flap should be about ¾ in from the sides of the cover. Baste the flaps in place.

4 Cut the bias tape or ribbon into 2 equal lengths. Fold each piece lengthwise and stitch close to the edges. Fold each tie in half and baste it to one corner of the patchwork, placing it along the seam joining the top and side borders with the fold even with the side edge and the ends toward the center.

5 Place the lining over the patchwork, enclosing all flaps and ties. Making sure that the side edges of the flaps and the free ends of the ties are not caught in the seam, baste and stitch the lining to the patchwork along the long sides, taking ½ in seam allowance.

6 Turn the cover right side out. Turn in the raw edges at top and bottom. This will bring the flap right side up. Baste the edges together and firmly slip-stitch the lining to the flap and the front seam allowance at top and bottom.

7 To join the patchwork and lining along the center, either tie them at the intersection of the blocks (see page 29) using crochet cotton, or work hand quilting around the center squares (see step 6, page 95).

8 Cut the nylon tape into 2 equal lengths. Separate the lengths and stitch one half to the underside of each flap, 1 in from the edge.

9 Place the cover on the sling and fold and pin the flaps over the ends. Mark the positions for the tape on the underside of the sling. (Allow a little ease for the cover.) Sew the strips of tape to the sling; or attach the tape with strong fabric glue.

10 Attach the cover with the nylon tape, and tie it loosely to the chair at the top.

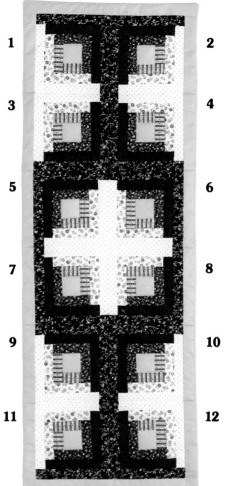

The arrangement of the numbered blocks in the correct order

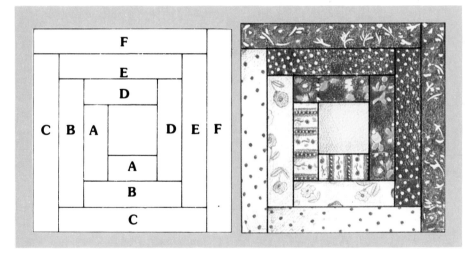

Diagram showing the arrangement of fabrics A - F in each block

The completed block showing the light-dark contrast of the fabrics

CURVED SHAPES

Some of the most charming patchwork designs include curved lines. Two such traditional favorites are "Grandmother's Fan" and "Double Wedding Ring", both of which lend themselves to the use of a wide assortment of fabric scraps. In the 19th century rich fabrics such as brocades were used, sometimes against a background of black satin, but both designs also work well with bright printed cottons, as the quilts shown here and on page 108 illustrate.

"Grandmother's Fan" is an easy design for beginners, and has the additional interest of combining patchwork, appliqué, and, if desired, embroidery. The fan itself is simply a quarter of a circle, divided into segments. The segments are joined and are then applied to a foundation square. If desired, embroidery stitches can then be added to decorate the fan. Lattice strips are often used to set the blocks; and the completed patchwork can then be quilted or tied, or used in some other way.

"Double Wedding Ring", by contrast, demands a certain degree of skill on the part of the maker if the circles are to be accurate. It is a good idea to start by making just one ring, using the sample for a throw pillow. The ring design is not decorated with embroidery stitches, but it does require quilting and is a good pattern for needleworkers who like to combine their patchwork and quilting skills.

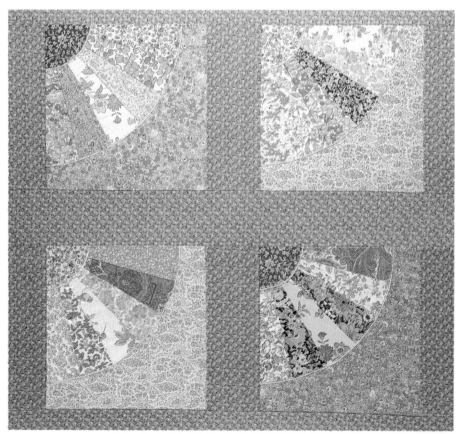

Both patterns are best used either as a single block made up into a pillow or in a large project such as a full-size quilt. Neither is well-suited to smaller projects, such as a baby's blanket, on which the patches would necessary be small and awkward to sew. On a larger scale, however, both patterns work well, and the results are extremely pleasing.

Fabrics for the "Double Wedding Ring" pattern should be of the best quality. This is because so many of the edges are cut on the bias, and cheap fabrics would tend to stretch and wrinkle when pieced together.

The pattern can be made from an assortment of prints and solid colors, with a different print used for each segment of the ring; or you may decide to select just a small number of fabrics that go well together, in order to produce a more controlled color scheme. It is essential that the fabrics all be of a similar visual strength, since any extreme contrast between light and dark will break up the ring pattern. However, the four squares placed where the rings link up often work best if cut from fabrics that contrast with the rings, giving additional interest to the design.

The background color may be light or dark. Dark backgrounds tend to make the colors more luminous and jewel-like, whereas lighter backgrounds expand the design and create a more airy feeling.

The larger of the background shapes, which occupies the center of each ring, is too big to be left unquilted. If you want to make a feature of the quilting it is best to choose a light, solid-colored fabric for the background, since this will show off the stitches. If you find quilting too time-consuming and want to do just the bare minimum to keep the batting in place, it is best to choose a fabric that has a small, busy pattern; in this case you need only quilt around the outlines of the rings.

For "Grandmother's Fan" lightweight fabrics are appropriate – at least for the pieces that are appliquéd onto the background fabric. Cotton lawn is a good choice for this kind of patchwork, although it is too fine for most other kinds.

Select a colorful variety of solid and printed fabrics for the fan shape, and use two different fabrics for the background square. These can be alternated when the blocks are joined. (Make sure, however, that the background fabric does not show through the fabrics of the fan shape.) The fabric for lattice strips, if used, should contrast with and complement the fabrics used for the blocks.

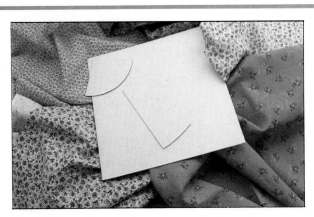

GRANDMOTHER'S FAN

1 Templates Three different templates are needed for the "Grandmother's Fan' pattern, A large square is used for the background to which the patches are applied. The fan is made up from patches cut to a wedge shape. The third template is for the corner from which the fan patches radiate. Because the wedge shape is used so many times, it is a good idea to cut several identical templates for it.

2 Preparing a block Mark and cut out all patches, placing one edge of the wedge-shaped template on the straight grain of the fabric. Piece 6 wedge-shaped patches together, press the seam allowances in one direction, and turn under and baste the seam allowance on the long curved edge. Also turn under and baste the seam allowance on the curved edge of the corner patch.

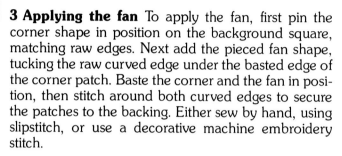

3 Applying the fan To apply the fan, first pin the corner shape in position on the background square, matching raw edges. Next add the pieced fan shape, tucking the raw curved edge under the basted edge of the corner patch. Baste the corner and the fan in position, then stitch around both curved edges to secure the patches to the backing. Either sew by hand, using slipstitch, or use a decorative machine embroidery stitch.

WEDDING RING

1 Templates Five templates are used in this pattern. Two – one larger and one smaller – are used for the background (mark the center point on each of these templates). Two shapes make up the arcs of the rings. One is symmetrical and the other, found at each end of each arc, is asymmetrical (beware of mixing these up). The fifth template is squarish., and is used for the four almost-square patches that connect every four arcs.

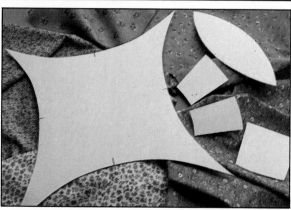

2 Marking and cutting To save time and avoid making mistakes, mark and cut all the pieces required for the project at one time. Use the marked center points to align the background templates with the lengthwise and crosswise grains of the fabric. Cut out the patches and transfer the center markings to them. The two small ring patches should be placed with one edge on the lengthwise grain. The asymmetrical patch is reversible (see step 3, page 81).

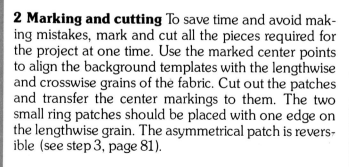
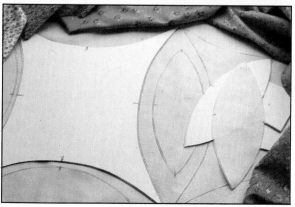

3 Making the arcs Basically the pattern is made from two pieced arcs, one of which has a squarish shape at each end. For the first arc, assemble symmetrical patches together and put an asymmetrical patch at each end, with the more sharply-angled straight edge on the outside. Sew the patches together and press the seams in one direction. Make another arc in the same way, then add a squarish shape at each end, so that the slightly curved side follows the outer curve of the arc.

4 Joining the arcs The two arcs are then assembled around one of the oval background patches. Attach the smaller arc first, matching the center points for accuracy and pinning before stitching. (You may also wish to baste these seams.) Attach the second arc, again matching the center points and pinning before stitching. Press the seam allowances away from the oval background shape. Clip the curves if necessary.

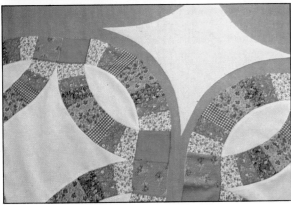

5 Making the rings Assemble 4 pieced leaf shapes around a large background patch, making sure, if you are using contrasting colors for the squarish shapes, that you have the correct juxtaposition of colors. Attach the leaf shapes one by one, carefully matching and pinning the center points before seaming them. The shapes should be attached in a clockwise direction. When the ring is complete, press the seam allowances away from the central background shape. Clip the curves if necessary.

6 Completing the pattern To complete the pattern, join the rings together, again using the large background shapes. First join them into rows, alternating rings with background shapes, then join the rows together in the same way. On the outside edges, add a pieced leaf shape to each of the joining background shapes to complete the ring effect, adding 2 of these at the corners.

RING AND FAN QUILTS

Both of these handsome traditional quilts incorporate curved shapes. The "Grandmother's Fan" design is the easier of the two, since there are fewer curves and the fan shape is appliquéd onto a background square. The "Double Wedding Ring" quilt is constructed entirely by piecing and requires some experience.

"Grandmother's Fan" quilt

1 Using graph paper, enlarge the pieces for the templates given below as specified. (See page 167.) Trace each piece separately and add $\frac{1}{4}$ in seam allowance to all edges. (Note that piece B is a complete square.)

2 Glue the tracings to the cardboard and cut out each template, using the craft knife – and the steel ruler on straight edges. Label the templates as on the pattern (the letters correspond to the fabrics used).

3 Cut out pieces for 35 fans as follows: template A, 210 patches; template B, 17 patches from one fabric and 18 from the other; template C. 17 patches from one fabric and 18 from the other; template D, 58 patches; template E, 24 patches. Keep the patches for each fan block together, making sure that the fan center is paired with the chosen background fabric in each case (see photograph).

4 To construct a block, begin by joining the 6 wedge sections. Lay them out in the preferred arrangement, then pin them together, with right sides facing. Baste (optional), then stitch the straight edges together, taking $\frac{1}{4}$ in seam allowance. Press all the seams to one side.

5 Turn under and baste $\frac{1}{4}$ in along the outer curved edge. Similarly, turn under and baste the curved edge of the corner piece (notch the edge, if necessary, to reduce bulk).

6 Place the corner piece in one corner of the background square, right sides upward and raw edges even; pin it in place. Add the fan piece, slipping the raw edge under the folded edge of the center piece and aligning the straight edges with the background square. Baste both pieces in place.

Templates (full size) for "fan" quilt

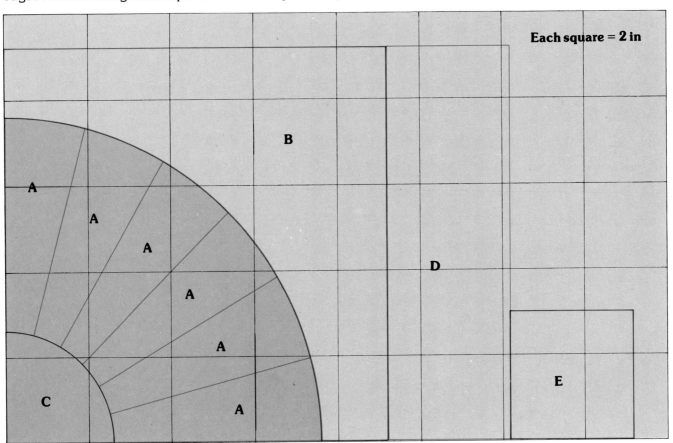

Each square = 2 in

Size

approximately 64 in by 87 in

You will need:

Assorted lightweight cotton fabrics, 36 in wide, in the following amounts:

Fabric A (an assortment of at least 6 different prints), 4 yd

Fabric B (2 similar prints for background squares), 2 yd

Fabric C (2 similar prints for quarter-circles), $\frac{1}{2}$ yd

Fabric D/E (small print for strips, borders, and backing), $6\frac{3}{8}$ yd
(If you wish to use cheaper fabric for the lining, subtract $4\frac{7}{8}$ yd from this amount)

Piece of flannelette, lightweight batting, or old blanket, 65 in by 88 in

Crochet cotton or other strong thread to match the patchwork colors, for tying

Chenille needle, sized 19 or 20

Graph paper

Tracing paper

Cardboard for templates

Steel ruler

Craft knife

Thread for embroidery, such as stranded floss (optional)

Sewing equipment and threads

7 Stitch along both curved edges, either by machine, using a close zigzag stitch, or by hand, using slipstitch. Or work embroidery stitches over the edges and the straight fan seams.

8 Assemble the remaining 34 blocks in the same way.

9 Join 5 blocks to 4 lattice strips to make one row, alternating the background colors as shown in the photograph and taking $\frac{1}{4}$ in seam allowance. Press the seams open. Make 6 more rows in the same way.

10 Join the remaining lattice strips to the small squares to make 6 strips the same length as the fan block rows. Press the seams open.

11 Join the rows and strips alternately to complete the patchwork. (The diagram below shows one-quarter of the patchwork, including borders.) Press the seams open.

12 From fabric D/E cut 4 border strips, each 5 in wide: 2 the length of the bottom and top edges of the patchwork and 2 the length of the side edges plus $9\frac{1}{2}$ in.

13 Pin, baste (optional), and stitch the shorter border strips to the top and bottom edges of the patchwork, placing right sides together and taking $\frac{1}{4}$ in seam allowance. Press.

14 Repeat step 13 to join the longer strips to the side edges. Press.

15 Cut the lining fabric in half widthwise, and join the two halves lengthwise. Trim the lining to the same size as the patchwork and flannelette.

16 Lay the lining right side down on the floor and place the flannelette on top. Pin and baste them together, working from the center outward (the basting lines need not be placed close together).

17 Place the patchwork and lining together, right sides facing, and pin and baste around the edges. Stitch, taking $\frac{1}{2}$ in seam allowance and leaving a 15 in gap in one side. Press the seam flat, grade the seam allowances (see page 167), and turn the quilt right side out. Turn in and baste the raw edges of the gap and slipstitch them together.

18 Pin the quilt layers together at widely-spaced intervals. Using the chenille needle and crochet cotton, tie the layers together at the four corners of each block (see page 29).

Diagram of one-quarter of "fan" quilt

"Double Wedding Ring" quilt

1 Trace the template patterns given on page 112. Note that template A is only one-quarter the full size and template E only one-half, so fold the tracing paper as required before tracing. All of the templates include ¼ in seam allowance.

2 Glue the template patterns to the cardboard and cut around them carefully with the craft knife. (If you are inexperienced in the use of a craft knife, cut the templates twice from thin cardboard, using scissors, and glue the two pieces together.) Label the templates as shown (the letters correspond to the fabrics used). Mark the center points on the A and E templates (see step 1, page 106).

3 Cut out patches as follows: template A, 20 patches; template B, 196 patches – 98 of them reversed (see step 3, page 81); template C, 558 patches; template D, 48 patches from fabric D¹ and 50 from fabric D²; template E, 49 patches.

4 Make an arc by joining 6 C patches as shown in step 3, page 107, then adding a B patch to each end. Make the remaining 97 arcs in the same way. Press the seam allowances to one side.

5 Join a D¹ patch to each end of 24 of the arcs and a D² patch to each end of 25 arcs. The remaining 49 arcs are left with just 8 pieces each.

6 Join one 8-patch arc to an oval E patch, matching the center seam to the center mark and basting before stitching. Join a 10-patch arc to this section, matching center seam to center point and making sure that the seams cross exactly at the corners. Press the two long seam allowances away from the center. Assemble 48 more oval shapes in the same way.

7 Join 4 of the oval shapes to an A patch, attaching them one by one in a clockwise direction and alternating the colors of the end patches as shown in step 5, page 107. When the ring is complete, press the seam allowances away from the center. Assemble 9 more rings in the same way.

8 Place the completed rings on the floor, alternating rows of 3 with rows of 2 and alternating the end patch colors as before (see photograph). Between each ring place one of the remaining E patches. Add an E patch to each end of the 2-ring rows, and add one of the 9 remaining oval shapes to the edges of these outer E patches to complete the patchwork arrangement. (The diagram at right shows one-quarter of the quilt.) Join the rings, E patches and ovals in rows, checking to make sure the order is correct; then join the rows to complete the patchwork. Press the work.

9 Using the fabric-marking pen, lightly mark the quilting lines as shown on the diagram. Begin with the line running diagonally between two corners, then add the other lines, keeping them parallel and about 2 in apart and continuing them into the small oval sections as shown.

10 Cut the lining fabric in half widthwise, then join the two halves lengthwise. Trim the piece to measure the same as the batting.

11 Pin the patchwork, batting, and lining fabric together and baste through the three layers, working from the center outward (see steps 2 and 3, page 13).

12 Quilt by machine (see page 30) along the marked straight lines.

13 Trim the batting and lining fabric to fit the edges of the patchwork and baste the edges together. Join the lengths of bias binding (see page 166), and pin, baste, and stitch one edge of the binding to the edge of the patchwork, taking ¼ in seam allowance. Press the binding away from the patchwork. Turn it to the underside. Fold under the raw edge and baste and slipstitch it to the lining fabric.

Size
approximately 71 in by 87 in

You will need:
Assorted lightweight cotton fabrics, 36 in wide, in the following amounts:

Fabric A/E (cream or white), 6½ yd

Fabric B/C (small prints in various colors) 5½ yd

Fabric D, ⅝ yd each of two harmonizing solid colors (called D¹ and D²)

5 yd of 45 in wide cotton fabric for lining

Piece of lightweight polyester batting about 75 in by 90 in

9¾ yd of purchased bias binding to match either color of fabric D

Cream or white quilting thread

Tracing paper

Cardboard for templates (see step 2)

Craft knife (optional)

Fabric-marking pen

Ruler

Sewing equipment and threads

Diagram of one-quarter of "ring" quilt showing positions of shapes and quilting lines

C

A

E

fold line

fold line

D

B

fold line

Templates (full size) for "ring" quilt

ENGLISH PATCHWORK

Unlike American patchwork, which typically consists of blocks formed by joining small units into progressively larger ones, English patchwork is structurally more uniform, rather like a mosaic. It may use two or three different shapes (which will entail a form of block construction), but many of the most popular deisgns consist of only one shape – the visual interest being created by the placement of the contrasting fabrics. "Grandmother's Flower Garden" (see page 117) is an example of this kind of design. It consists entirely of hexagons – a favorite English patchwork shape – arranged in rosettes made from different fabrics, which are separated by "paths" of hexagons in a unifying background color.

English patchwork also differs from American patchwork in that it is always sewn by hand. Each patch is basted to a paper shape, the size of the finished patch, and then the patches are sewn together along their adjacent sides, using tiny overcasting stitches and working through the fabric only. The paper shapes are then removed.

Clamshell patchwork (see page 119) is a variation of this basic method. In this type of patchwork the shapes are overlapped, then basted together and joined with slipstitch.

Although it is necessarily time-consuming, English patchwork is an enjoyable craft for anyone who likes hand-sewing. It is a very accurate method of patchwork and is ideally suited to designs involving curved lines.

Fabrics used for English patchwork should be fairly lightweight, so that you can follow the shape of the backing paper when turning and basting the patch to it. If you want to use a finer fabric – either by itself or mixed with slightly heavier ones – first apply iron-on interfacing to the wrong side, to give it extra body and make it opaque. If different weights of fabric are combined the heavier ones will tend to pull the lighter ones out of shape.

Even more than in other forms of patchwork it is important that the fabrics crease easily, especially if sharp angles (such as on diamonds) are involved. And, of course, the fabrics should not be stretchy or fray easily.

Thread and needles Sew with a good-quality cotton-polyester thread of a neutral color; run the thread through a cake of beeswax to prevent it from twisting. Quilting thread, if available, will give extra strength to the work.

Use a size 9 or 10 sharp or betweens needle for joining the patches. For pinning the patches to the backing papers, use fine silk pins.

Templates for the main English patchwork shapes – hexagons, diamonds, octagons – are available in needlework shops and are made of aluminum so that they will not wear out; however, you may not find one of the size you want. In this case, you will need to make your own from cardboard.

If you are making your own templates, you may also need a compass, a right-angled triangle, a protractor for measuring angles, a well-sharpened pencil, a steel ruler, and a craft knife.

The backing papers may be cut from brown paper, as shown, or from any fairly stiff paper such as old greeting cards or the covers of magazines.

1 Designing It is easiest to plan simple one-patch patterns by arranging the fabrics into light and dark colors. If it is difficult to decide into which category a printed fabric falls, half close your eyes to eliminate some of the detail. Group fabrics that go well together and ones that show interesting contrasts. Intricate designs should first be worked out on isometric graph paper with felt-tipped pens.

2 Making a hexagon template If your design uses hexagons and you cannot find one the right size, you can make your own. Set the compass to the same length as one side of the hexagon. Draw a circle on thick cardboard. Keeping the compass to the same width, place the point anywhere on the circumference and draw a small arc crossing the circle. Move the point to that arc and draw another. Repeat until there are 6 intersections, then join the points, using a ruler and a sharp, hard pencil. Add a ¼ in seam allowance on all sides and cut out the template. Make another template without the seam allowance.

3 Window templates These are used to frame part of a patterned fabric so that a patch can be cut with a motif exactly in the center or a geometric print can be positioned at just the right angle. Make the template as shown, adding the seam allowance but cutting around the inner sewing line as well as the outer cutting line, to make a frame. The inner shape can be used for marking out backing papers. This type of template is very useful, but it is not so strong as the solid kind so it may be better to make one of each.

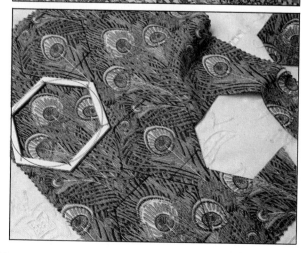

4 Backing papers A paper pattern is needed to shape each individual patch. These must be cut accurately if the patches are to fit together correctly. Place the smaller template on brown paper and carefully trace around the edge with a hard pencil. Make a paper for each patch. A quick alternative is to mark out as many as will fit on a sheet of paper and make photocopies. Cut out each shape, taking care to cut accurately; ideally, use a metal ruler and craft knife.

5 Cutting the fabric Mark the fabric on the wrong side with a sharp, colored pencil. Use the larger template (either a window template or a solid one) and keep the top and bottom of the template parallel to the crosswise grain of the fabric. Mark and cut each shape individually, leaving no space between patches. When using selected parts of a patterned fabric, place the window template on the right side of the fabric to frame the area and mark only around the outside edge.

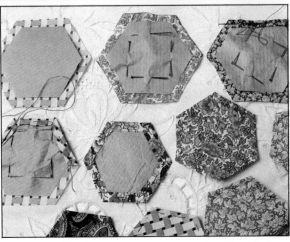

6 Preparing to sew Center and pin the backing paper to the wrong side of the fabric patch, making sure that the edges of the backing paper and the fabric are parallel. Fold the fabric over the paper shape, one edge at a time, and secure it with basting stitches. Begin and end with backstitches (not a knot) for ease in removing the stitches later. Fold the fabric carefully at the corners to retain the shape. When the basting is complete, press the patch on both sides to sharpen the sewing edge.

7 Joining patches Place the patches together with right sides facing and join them with small, even overcasting stitches, trying not to sew through the backing papers. Make sure the corners match, keeping them together with a pin if necessary. Start by pushing the needle through at the corner of a patch, underneath the fabric, and begin and end with several backstitches. When assembling a rosette, start with the center patch and join it to one of the outer patches, then add the remaining five hexagons, working clockwise. Then join the second row of hexagons, working in the same direction.

8 Finishing Either leave the edge as it is, following the shape made by the hexagons, and sew on a separate binding or add extra half and quarter shapes to straighten the edges, sewing on the patches in the same way as for the full hexagons. When all the patches have been joined, pull out the basting stitches and remove the backing papers. These can be re-used if they are unmarked. Press the patchwork first on the wrong side and then on the right side, using a pressing cloth.

ENGLISH PATCHWORK

"GRANDMOTHER'S FLOWER GARDEN" QUILT

An assortment of solid-color and printed fabrics is used for the rosettes in this appealing quilt, based on a traditional English design. The bright yellow flower centers and cool green background unify the contrasting colors of the motifs.

Size
approximately 73 in by 79 in

You will need:
Dressweight cotton fabrics, 36 in wide, in the following amounts:

Fabric A (rosette centers), ½ yd

Fabric B (assorted prints), 2¾ yd (total)

Fabric C (assorted solid colors), 5 yd (total)

Fabric D (borders), 4 yd

4⅛ yd of lightweight cotton fabric, at least 39 in wide, for lining

Piece of lightweight polyester batting 76 in by 83 in (approx.)

14 yd of ½ in-wide single fold bias binding

Tracing paper

Cardboard for templates

Steel ruler

Craft knife

Medium-stiff paper for backing papers

Sewing equipment and threads, including quilting thread

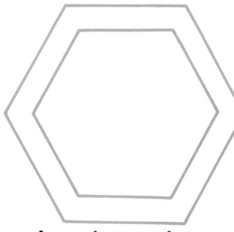

Inner and outer templates, full size

Making the patchwork
1 Trace the hexagon shapes given here – both the larger and the smaller. Use the tracings as patterns to cut an inner and an outer template from the cardboard, using the steel ruler and craft knife. If some of the printed fabrics need to be cut with the design positioned in a certain way, you should also make a window template. For this, trace the hexagon shape exactly as given here, and cut out the smaller shape to leave a window in the larger one.

2 Using the small, solid template, cut 500 paper patches (these can be re-used as work progresses). Be careful to draw very close to the edge, using a sharp pencil or fine pen. When a template becomes worn, make another one.

3 Using the larger template (and the window template, if required), cut fabric patches as follows: Fabric A (rosette centers), 68 patches; Fabric B (assorted prints), 408 patches, in groups of 6 each; Fabric C (assorted solid colors), 816 patches, in groups of 12 each; Fabric D (borders), 742 patches. Keep the patches for each rosette together.

4 Pin and baste a patch to each backing paper, as shown in step 6, page 115, taking care to keep the corners as neat and sharp as possible. Prepare at least enough patches for a rosette before beginning to sew the patches together. Press each patch on both sides.

5 To make a rosette, begin by joining one of the printed patches to one side of the center patch, using tiny overcasting stitches, as shown in step 7, page 116. Join another printed patch to the next side (working clockwise) of the center patch. Then join the adjacent sides of the two printed patches. Continue in the same way until all of the printed patches have been joined to the center patch and to each other.

6 Now add the solid-color patches in the same way to complete the rosette. Make 67 more rosettes in the same way.

7 Arrange the rosettes in 9 rows, alternating 5 rows of 8 rosettes with 4 rows of 7. Join the rows of the rosettes one by one, linking each pair of rosettes with 2 border hexagons, placed side by side. Then link the rows, putting a band of border hexagons between each. A single band of hexagons runs across the 9 rows, and a double band runs along the two outer rows of 8 rosettes. Press the completed patchwork, opening the outer seam allowances so that they lie flat. Remove the papers.

Quilting
1 Cut the lining fabric in half widthwise and join the two halves lengthwise.

2 Place the lining fabric, right side down, on the floor. Lay the piece of batting on top, and place the patchwork on top, centering it and making sure that all three layers are smooth. Do not trim the lining or batting.

3 Pin the layers together over the entire surface, then baste them together, working from the center outward (see steps 2 and 3, page 13).

4 Quilt around the inner edge of each hexagon, ¼ in from the seam, using quilting thread and a fine running stitch. (The work can be placed in a quilting frame or hoop, if you like.)

5 Trim the lining fabric and batting to the same size as the patchwork. Pin and baste the bias binding to the edges of the patchwork, with right sides facing and edges matching. Machine stitch ¼ in from the raw edge. Press the seam flat.

6 Turn the binding over to the underside. Pin and baste the remaining folded edge to the lining, then slipstitch it in place.

CLAMSHELL PATCHWORK ACCESSORIES

Possibly the trickiest to handle of all patchwork shapes, the clam-shell is also one of the prettiest — as these throw pillows and tea cozy demonstrate. Many interesting patterns can be created using contrasting solid colors and prints. Select fine, soft cottons (or silks, if you are experienced), and work as accurately as possible.

Tea cozy
Size
12¼ in by 10 in

You will need:

5 different fabrics (fine, closely-woven cottons), 36 in wide, in the following amounts:

Fabric A (green), ½ yd

Fabric B (bright pink), ¼ yd

Fabric C (print), ¼ yd

Fabric D (blue), ⅛ yd

Fabric E (pale pink), ⅛ yd

28 in of ⅛ in-diameter filler cord

⅜ yd of soft cotton lining fabric

⅜ yd of 36 in-wide lightweight, non-woven, sew-in interfacing

⅜ yd of 36 in-wide lightweight polyester batting

Tracing paper

Cardboard for templates (see step 1)

Craft knife (optional)

Stiff paper for clamshell shapes

Fabric-marking pen

Cork mat or other soft board slightly larger than patchwork

Piece of flat elastic about 12 in long

2 thumbtacks

Graph paper

Sewing equipment and threads

Inner and outer templates, full size

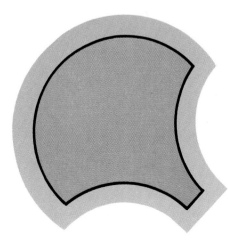

Tea cozy

1 Trace both the inner and the outer clamshell shapes given below. Use the tracings to cut the two templates from stiff cardboard, using a craft knife; or, if you are not skilled in the use of a knife, cut two each from thin cardboard, using scissors, and glue them together. Also make a window template, if desired.

2 Using the smaller template, cut about 10 or 12 clamshell shapes from stiff paper.

3 Using the larger template (and the window template, if desired, for the printed fabric), cut patches as follows: fabric A, 42 patches; fabric B, 22 patches; fabric C, 24 patches; fabric D, 12 patches; fabric E, 6 patches. (The tea cozy shown uses part of fabric C here.) Divide each group in half, so that you have one set of patches for each side of the tea cozy.

4 To prepare a patch, place one of the stiff paper shapes on the wrong side of a fabric patch. Center it exactly and pin it in place as shown opposite. Fold the upper curved edge of the fabric over the paper. Using a fine needle and thread, baste through the seam allowance only, making tiny stitches and gathering the fabric smoothly. Fasten off securely. Remove the pins, press the turned edge, and remove the paper shape. Prepare all the patches in this way.

5 Place the top 2 patches (fabric C) on the cork mat, right side up and side by side, with the edges touching. To make sure that they lie straight, place the elastic across them, ¼ in above the straight lower edges. Stretch it slightly to give a straight line, then pin the ends to the board. Adjust the clamshells, if necessary, and pin them to the board.

6 Place the next row – 3 clamshells – (see photograph) on top of the first row, with their folded edges overlapping the ¼ in seam allowances of the first two; check their alignment with the elastic, as before. Pin them in place.

7 Taking care not to move the clamshells, baste them together through the overlapped seam allowances. Remove them from the board and slipstitch them together, taking tiny stitches.

8 Place the patchwork on the board again, and join the third row in the same way. Continue in this way until one side of the patchwork is complete. (If you prefer, you can pin down the entire shape at once, then baste and sew the pieces together.)

9 Join the remaining pieces in the same way to make the other side of the tea cozy. Press the patchwork.

10 On graph paper draw a pattern for the tea cozy shape, using the dimensions shown on the photograph, opposite. Cut the shape twice from interfacing. Then cut it from the following fabrics, adding ½ in seam allowance to the edges each time : 2 pieces of green backing fabric, 6 pieces of lining fabric, and 2 pieces of batting.

11 Baste each piece of patchwork to the right side of a green piece. Trim the edges of the patchwork even with the backing. Slipstitch the interfacing to the wrong side of the backing.

12 From the green fabric, cut and join enough 1¾ in-wide bias strips (see page 166) to cover the filler cord. Cut a small piece on the straight grain, 1 in by 4 in. Cover the cord as shown on page 166. Fold the small piece in half lengthwise, right sides together, and stitch ¼ in from the edges. Trim the seam and turn the tube right side out. Press.

13 Pin and baste the cording to the patchwork side of one section, along the side and top edges, with the stitching ½ in from the edge and the cord

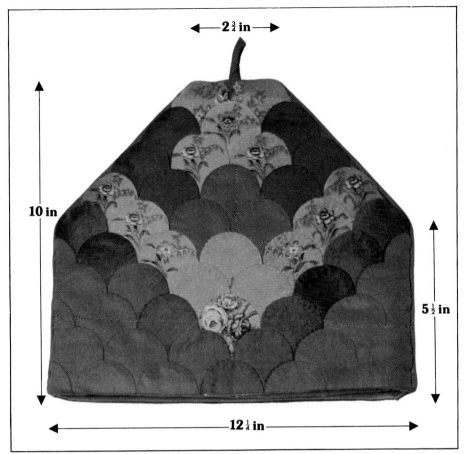

Measurements shown: 2¾ in (top), 10 in (left height), 12¼ in (bottom width), 5½ in (right).

Tracing the stiff paper shapes

Making a window template

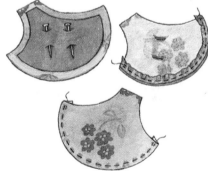

Preparing a patch

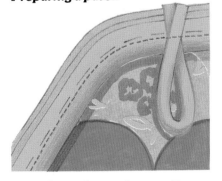

Attaching the cording and loop

toward the center. Fold the tube to form a loop and baste it in the center, with the loop pointing inward. (See the diagram below.)

14 Baste the other section on top, right sides facing. Using the zipper foot on the machine, stitch close to the cord. Grade the seam allowances and trim the cord ends even with the lower edge.

15 Pin and baste the interfacing pieces to the front and back of the cover. Sew them in place using herringbone stitch. Turn up and press the seam allowance around the lower edge.

16 Place 2 lining pieces together, right sides facing. Pin and stitch along the side and top edges. Trim the seam.

17 Turn the patchwork cover right side out. Leaving the lining wrong side out, slip it into the cover and secure it with a couple of pins at the top. Turn up the raw edges so that they lie between the cover and the lining and so that the folded edges are even. Baste, then slipstitch them together. Turn the cover wrong side out and baste the lining in place at the top.

18 To make the inner, removable pad, first place 2 lining pieces together, right sides facing. Trim away the seam allowance on the lower edge only of the batting pieces. Sandwich the lining pieces between the batting pieces. Pin, baste, and stitch along the side and top edges. Trim the seam close to the stitching and turn the piece right side out.

19 Join the remaining pieces of lining and insert this piece, wrong side out, into the padded piece. Turn in the lower edges on both pieces, and baste and slipstitch them together. Place the patchwork cover over the pad.

Size

12 in square

You will need:

3 different fabrics (fine, closely-woven cottons), 36 in wide, in the following amounts:

Fabric A (solid color – here, bright pink), ½ yd

Fabric B (medium-size print), ⅝ yd

Fabric C (small-size print), ⅜ yd

50 in of ⅛ in-diameter filler cord

Pillow form 13 in square (larger than cover for a plump shape)

Tracing paper

Cardboard (see step 1 of "Tea cozy") for templates

Craft knife (optional)

Stiff paper for clamshell shapes

Cork mat or other soft board slightly larger than patchwork

Piece of flat elastic about 12 in long

2 thumbtacks

Sewing equipment and threads

Square pillow

1 Cut the templates and about 5 or 6 paper clamshell shapes, following steps 1 and 2 of "Tea cozy."

2 Using the larger template (and a window template, if desired), cut patches as follows: fabric A, 12 patches; fabric B, 28 patches; fabric C, 20 patches.

3 Prepare the patches as described in step 4 of "Tea cozy."

4 Join the patches as described in steps 5 – 8 of "Tea cozy," but following the arrangement shown in the photograph of the square pillow, making 4 identical triangular shapes. Press the patchwork.

5 Cut 2 pieces of backing from fabric A, each 13¼ in square. Baste the pieces of patchwork to the right side of one square, centering them carefully. Trim away the lower edges of the bottom rows of clamshells.

6 Cut and join enough 2 in-wide bias strips of fabric A to cover the filler cord (see page 166). Wrap the bias strip around the cord and stitch close to it.

7 Pin the cording to the right side of the patchwork, with the stitching ⅝ in from the raw edge (i.e. so that the cord lies outside the seam allowance) and the ends overlapped smoothly. Baste it in place.

8 Place the other square on top of the patchwork with right sides facing; baste around the edges. Using the zipper foot of the machine, stitch ⅝ in from the raw edges, as close as possible to the cord, leaving a gap of about 7 in in one side (not the side with the overlapped ends of cording).

9 Grade the seam allowances (see page 167) and turn the pillow cover right side out. Insert the pillow form. Turn in the raw edge of the backing and slip-stitch it to the cording.

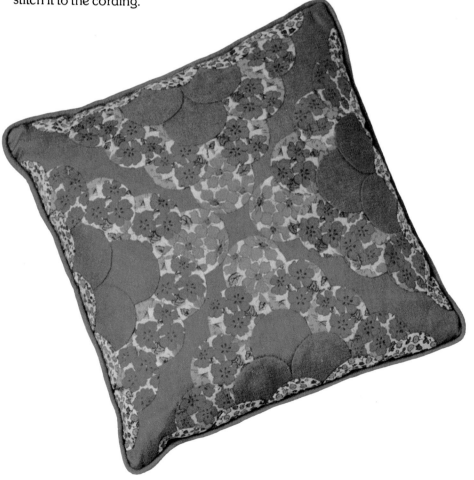

Oblong pillow

1 Cut the templates and 5 or 6 paper clamshell shapes, following steps 1 and 2 of "Tea cozy."

2 Using the larger template (and a window template, if desired), cut patches as follows: fabric A, 8 patches; fabric B, 8 patches; fabric C, 30 patches; fabric D, 16 patches.

3 Prepare the patches as described in step 4 of "Tea cozy."

4 Following the arrangement shown in the photograph, make two pieces of patchwork, using the method described in steps 5 – 8 of "Tea cozy." Press the patchwork.

5 Cut a strip of fabric A, 10 in by 2½ in. Baste the upper edge of each patchwork piece to the right side of the strip, so that the scalloped edges just touch, as shown. Slipstitch the edges in place.

6 Cut 2 strips of fabric B, each 10 in by 2 in. Join one long edge of each strip to the lower edges of the patchwork, taking ⅜ in seam allowance. Trim the lower edges of the clamshell even with the fabric strip. Press the seam away from the patchwork.

7 Cut a rectangle of fabric B the same size as the completed patchwork.

8 Cut and join enough 2 in-wide bias strips of fabric A to cover the filler cord (see page 166). Wrap the bias strip around the cord and stitch close to it.

9 Using the fabric-marking pen and a ruler, draw the seamline on the right side of the patchwork; it should just touch the outer corners of the fabric A and fabric B patches and run ⅜ in from the raw edges at each end.

10 Pin the cording to the right side of the patchwork, with the stitching just over the marked seamline and the cord lying outside the seam allowance. Overlap the ends smoothly on one long side. Baste the cording in place.

11 Place the backing piece on top of the patchwork with right sides facing; baste around the edges. Using the zipper foot of the machine, stitch close to the cord, leaving a gap of about 7 in in one short end.

12 Grade the seam allowances and turn the pillow cover right side out.

13 Make the pillow form: cut 2 pieces of unbleached muslin, each 10 in by 18½ in. Pin and stitch them together around the edges, taking ½ in seam allowance and leaving a 5 in gap in one side. Turn the pillow right side out and stuff it firmly with the fiberfill. Slipstitch the opening edges together.

14 Insert the pillow form into the cover. Turn in the raw edge of the backing and slipstitch it to the cording.

Size
16½ in by 8 in

You will need:

4 different fabrics (fine, closely-woven cottons), 36 in wide, in the following amounts:

Fabric A (green), ⅛ yd

Fabric B (bright pink), ⅜ yd

Fabric C (print), ¼ yd

Fabric D (pale pink), ⅛ yd

52 in of ⅛ in-diameter filler cord

½ yd of unbleached muslin, any width

Fiberfill for stuffing

Tracing paper

Cardboard (see step 1 of "Tea cozy") for templates

Craft knife (optional)

Stiff paper for clamshell shapes

Cork mat or other soft board slightly larger than patchwork

Piece of flat elastic about 12 in long

2 thumbtacks

Fabric-marking pen

Sewing equipment and threads

CRAZY PATCHWORK

Crazy patchwork is a random mixture of fabric scraps stitched, in haphazard fashion, to a background fabric. The patches can be of any size, shape, color, pattern, or texture. The important thing is that no two patches be alike and that there be no set pattern in which they are arranged. The finished patchwork is seldom quilted, but may instead be tied at intervals to a lining fabric. If it used for a quilt, lightweight batting may be included.

Originally, crazy patchwork was a means of putting every scrap of spare fabric to good use. These might be left over from dressmaking, or salvaged from usable parts of worn-out clothing. In the late 1800s, when the fashion for crazy patchwork was at its height, the fabrics used were luxurious ones — satins, brocades, and velvets — and they were lavishly embroidered, both along the edges and, frequently, in the center as well.

Today the taste for such ornate work has declined, but crazy patchwork is still enjoyed for its delightfully eccentric appearance and striking contrast of textures. Because the fabrics are stitched to a backing (usually unbleached muslin), it is possible to combine weights and textures that could never work together in other kinds of patchwork.

Although the essence of the craft is its random look, it is a good idea to do a little planning before you begin cutting and stitching. Make a rough sketch to decide how you would like the shapes to relate to each other, and use colored pencils or felt-tips to indicate the placement of different fabrics, so that you don't end up with an unbalanced color scheme. You can then use this sketch as a guide and simply cut patches freehand, as shown in step 1, opposite.

An alternative is to make a full-size pattern (the method used for the play mat on page 127), transfer the design to the backing fabric, then cut up the pattern and use the pieces to cut the individual patches.

Fabrics You will need fabrics in a wide variety of weights and textures; usually the more you use, the richer the look and feel of the finished item will be. If you are using an existing stock of fabric scraps, you will need to plan your design around these quantities; if you are buying new fabrics, you must roughly measure the area of each piece (multiplying height by width and remembering to increase these proportionately if your design is not full-size), then add up these measurements to get the total area. Add 25 percent for seam allowances and trimming.

For backing, buy unbleached muslin the size of the finished patchwork.

Depending on the item you are making, you may also need lining fabric and lightweight batting.

Threads and needles If you are stitching the patches by machine, using zigzag stitch as shown here, you will need ordinary sewing threads in appropriate colors. Use silk thread for a richer effect. If you are working hand embroidery over the edges you will need embroidery floss, pearl cotton, or other suitable thread, and a crewel or chenille needle.

Materials for transferring the design Cardboard templates are not used for crazy patchwork, but if you are working out a full-size design you will need a large sheet of paper and some dressmaker's carbon for transferring the design. If you are enlarging a design, you will also need graph paper.

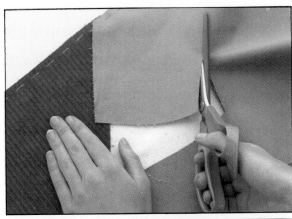

1 Applying the first patch Cut the first patch to fit one corner of the backing. Pin and baste it in place along the two outer edges. Next, place the fabric for the adjacent patch on the backing so that it overlaps the edge of the first patch by $\frac{3}{4}$ in and is even with the edge of the backing. Note: If you are cutting all patches in advance, simply add $\frac{3}{8}$ in (the net seam allowance) to each edge.

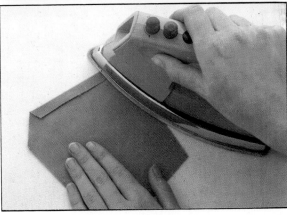

2 Pressing Turn under and press $\frac{3}{8}$ in on the edge that will overlap the edge of the first patch. If the turned edge leaves a mark on the right side when pressed, slip a piece of cardboard between it and the rest of the fabric when pressing. Subsequent patches will need two or more edges pressed: cut away excess fabric at corners to miter them, and if the fabric frays, apply iron-on interfacing to secure these corner edges.

3 Applying the second patch Pin and baste the second patch in place, overlapping the edge of the first patch by $\frac{3}{8}$ in. Baste along the outer edges also. (Note that when you cut a patch you should allow $\frac{3}{8}$ in extra on an edge that will be overlapped by another patch and $\frac{3}{4}$ in where the edge will be turned under.

4 Subsequent patches Cut and apply the third patch in the same way (here, two edges have $\frac{3}{4}$ in added and are turned under $\frac{3}{8}$ in). Continue adding patches until the entire piece of backing is covered.

5 Stitching To machine stitch the patches in place, use a close zigzag stitch and work over the turned edges. A machine embroidery stitch can be used instead, if desired.

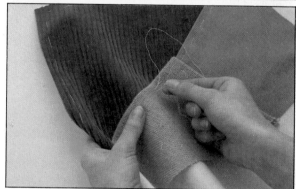

6 Embroidery Alternatively, work hand embroidery over the edges. Herringbone stitch and feather stitch are two of the most suitable. If the fabric is loosely woven, make the stitches wider and work them close together.

LANDSCAPE PLAY MAT

This crazy patchwork play mat uses a clever assortment of fabrics to suggest plowed fields, pasture, various crops, water, and other features of a rural landscape.

Size
40 in by 60 in

You will need:

⅛ yd each of 8 different fabrics, any width, for "field" areas of mat – for example: velveteen, various weights of corduroy, terry cloth, fleece

Piece of blue moiré 1 yd by 12 in

Piece of lightweight iron-on interfacing the same size as moiré

1 yd of 60 in-wide brown tweed fabric

1¾ yd of unbleached muslin 45 in wide

Graph paper

Dressmaker's carbon

Tracing paper

Silicon dirt repellent spray (optional)

Sewing equipment and threads

Making the patchwork

1 Using graph paper (several pieces taped together, if necessary), enlarge the pattern on page 129 as specified. (See page 167).

2 Using dressmaker's carbon, transfer the lines of the enlarged design to the piece of unbleached muslin. Also trace the outline of the patchwork area (inside the borders).

3 Label your fabrics A, B, and so on, and keep labeled scraps of the fabrics handy for reference. Label their positions on the muslin backing also. Cut up the enlarged pattern and label each pattern piece with the letter corresponding to the appropriate fabric. Keep the pieces for each fabric together.

4 Cut the pattern pieces for the fields from the appropriate fabrics, adding ⅜ in seam allowance to all edges and – in the case of the corduroy patches – making sure that the grain will run in various directions on the completed map. (Check the design.) From the blue moiré, cut the pieces for the river and pond, adding seam allowances only to the ends. Cut these pieces in interfacing also. Cut the roads (including seam allowances) from the tweed fabric.

5 Beginning at one corner, pin and baste each piece to the appropriate place on the background fabric, as shown in steps 1-6, pages 126-127 Stitch along the edges of each piece, either by machine, using zigzag stitch, or by hand, using feather or herringbone stitch. (Do not turn under seam allowances along edges of roads or water.)

6 When all the field pieces have been attached, add the pond and river. First iron the interfacing pieces to the wrong side of each piece. Then pin, baste, and stitch the pieces in place (leaving the seam allowances flat).

7 Apply the roads as for the field pieces, turning under seam allowances as required. Apply the four "vertical" roads first; then apply the two "horizontal" roads, overlapping the ends of the previously-applied roads.

Finishing the mat

1 Trim the lining so that the edges extend ¼ in beyond the patchwork.

2 From the remaining tweed fabric cut 4 strips, each 5 in wide, 2 measuring 61½ in and 2 measuring 41½ in. Trace the pattern given on this page, and use this to shape each end of each strip.

3 Pin and baste the strips together at the corners, with right sides facing, and stitch, taking ⅝ in seam allowance. Trim each seam and clip it at the inner points. Press the seams open and turn the border right side out.

4 Pin one edge of the border to the underside of the mat, with right sides facing and raw edges matching. Baste and stitch, taking ⅝ in seam allowance.

5 Turn the border to the right side. Turn under the ⅝ in seam allowance and baste the folded edge over the patchwork edges. Stitch by machine or by hand. Press.

6 Spray both sides of the mat with silicon dirt repellent, if desired. Use the spray again after each cleaning.

Trace pattern for border corners

Pattern for rug

SOMERSET PATCHWORK

Also known as "folded star," because of the star-shaped patterns it produces, Somerset patchwork is a relatively quick and easy technique which involves more folding then sewing. The patches are formed from rectangles, which are folded into triangles and then attached to a backing fabric.

A finished piece of Somerset patchwork is usually round or square, with the patches radiating out to the edge of the design or framed by a separate border. The design may cover just a small area and be used for the top of a box, a pot holder, or a Christmas tree ornament; or it may be extended to make a pillow cover or a wall hanging. As a rule, Somerset patchwork is best restricted to items that are mainly, or purely, decorative, for the lapped folds of fabric make it less hard-wearing than other forms of patchwork.

Its main advantage – apart from the pretty designs – is that it is so easy. And because it is so quick, it is ideal for anyone who wants to make small gifts for Christmas or birthdays and who does not have much time to spare.

Fabrics suitable for Somerset patchwork are essentially the same as for other forms of patchwork. They should be lightweight and should take a crease well: dressweight cottons are ideal. Printed fabrics add interest to these designs – but be sure to keep them small-scale, or they will detract from the design.

Selecting the fabrics is the first stage of designing Somerset patchwork – the formal arrangement of patches being decided after the patches are cut. Buy a small amount ($\frac{1}{8}$ to $\frac{1}{4}$ yd) of about 6 to 10 fabrics (depending on the size of the project) and experiment with them as described in step 4.

The backing fabric should be of cotton and in a light color, so that it can be easily marked; unbleached muslin is a good choice.

Thread should be a cotton-polyester or (if you are using silk fabrics) a fine silk, and it should match the fabric colors as closely as possible.

Other equipment You will need the usual equipment for making the template (see page 52). A fine fabric-marking pen is used for marking the backing, and a compass is useful for drawing borders. A steam iron is essential for accurate pressing.

1 Making the template Only one rectangular-shaped template is required for Somerset patchwork. The size may vary according to the design but the proportions must be correct, the template being 2 squares wide plus a $\frac{1}{4}$ in seam allowance along one long edge. Avoid making the patches too small and fiddly or too large and clumsy – a rectangle should generally measure between $1\frac{1}{4}$ in by $2\frac{1}{2}$ in and $1\frac{3}{4}$ in by $3\frac{1}{2}$ in excluding the seam allowance.

2 Preparing the patches Mark and cut out the patches. To prepare a patch, place it wrong side up and turn up a ¼ in allowance along one long edge. Press it flat. Mark the center point of the opposite edge, then bring the two corners at each end of the folded edge down to meet at this central point, making a sharp point at the top edge. Press the patch carefully, making sure that the two folded edges meet down the center (this side is now the front).

3 Designing First prepare the backing fabric. Cut it slightly larger than the finished work, and divide it into 8 equal sections (see step 4). Then prepare 8 patches each of your chosen fabrics. Arrange them in a number of ways to reveal the various design possibilities. Make a rough, annotated sketch of the chosen design for reference later. Note that the following steps are for a round-shaped project, but the basic techniques can easily be adapted to fit square or rectangular shapes.

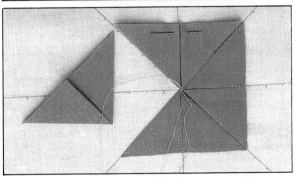

4 The first round Take 4 patches of the same color and pin the first to the backing fabric with the point to the center and the folded sides lying on penciled lines. Secure the point with a small neat stitch worked from the back through all layers. Make 3 more stitches, one stitch on each side and one in the center, ⅛ in to ¼ in up from the raw edge. Attach the other 3 patches in the same way, making sure that they meet exactly at the center.

5 The second round Take 8 patches of another color for the second round. Pin and tack the first four of these in position. All patches should be the same distance out from the center, and the points should align with those of the center 4. Next, add the remaining patches, again checking that they are all the same distance from the center. The second 4 patches overlap the first 4 of the second round.

6 The third round For the third round take another 8 patches, again of a different color. Place these in between the patches of the previous round so that the points of the patches touch the outer points of the star shape made by the first round. Pin and sew the patches in place as described in step 5.

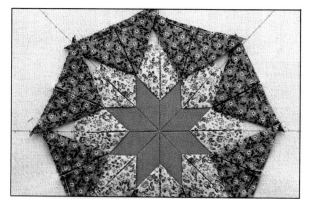

7 The fourth round Take another 8 patches, again of a different color. Position these in the same way as the patches of the second round, pinning the first 4 to align with 4 patches in the second round and then pinning the next 4 patches so that they align with the other 4 patches of the second round and overlap the first 4 patches of this round. Continue in this way for the remaining rounds, doubling the number of patches per round as necessary, according to the design.

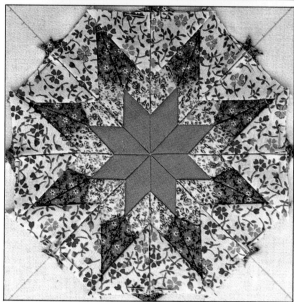

8 Borders To add a border, cut a piece of border fabric to the same size as the backing. Measure the diameter of the patchwork to be shown and, using the compass, draw a circle this size on the back of the border fabric. Stitch around this circle, then cut out an inner circle, $\frac{3}{8}$ in from the stitched line. Clip almost up the line, fold the raw edge to the wrong side and baste. Position the border over the patchwork, right side up, and pin, baste, and stitch around the inner circle.

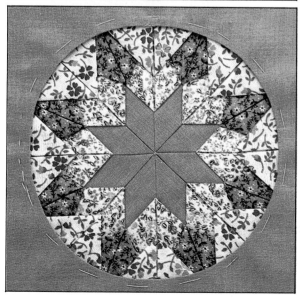

SOMERSET PATCHWORK PILLOWS

These two pretty pillows are easily made using the Somerset patchwork technique and a selection of harmonizing prints and solid colors in shades of peach and periwinkle blue – or whatever colors you like.

Peach pillow

1 Using the steel ruler and craft knife, cut a cardboard template 1½ in by 2½ in (this includes ¼ in seam allowance).

2 Use this template to cut the following patches: fabric A, 16 patches; fabric B, 24 patches; fabric C, 20 patches; fabric D, 16 patches; fabric E, 24 patches.

3 Cut the backing fabric to measure 18 in square. Using the fabric-marking pen and ruler, divide it into quarters and then into eighths. Mark each line at ½ in intervals. You may prefer to do Somerset patchwork in an embroidery hoop; if so, cut the backing to fit the hoop.

4 Fold and press each patch as shown in step 2, page 131.

Peach pillow
Size
approximately 16 in diameter

You will need:

5 different lightweight cotton fabrics, 36 in wide, in the following amounts:

Fabric A (light peach), $\frac{7}{8}$ yd

Fabric B (peach and yellow print), $\frac{5}{8}$ yd

Fabric C (beige), $\frac{1}{4}$ yd

Fabric D (peach and green print), $\frac{1}{4}$ yd

Fabric E (dark peach), $\frac{3}{8}$ yd

$\frac{1}{2}$ yd of unbleached muslin, any width, for backing

50 in of $\frac{3}{16}$ in-diameter filler cord

Round pillow form, 16 in in diameter (or unbleached muslin and fiberfill for making one)

12 in zipper

Cardboard for template

Steel ruler

Craft knife

Compass

Colored pencil or fabric-marking pen

Sewing equipment and threads

5 Pin and tack the patches to the backing fabric as shown in step 4, page 131, in the following order:

Round 1 Attach 4 patches of fabric A, making sure that the points meet accurately in the center.

Round 2 Take 8 patches of fabric B and place the first 4 between the patches in the first round and the remaining patches between these. The points should be $\frac{1}{2}$ in out from the center of the work.

Round 3 Take 4 patches of A and 4 of C and place them, alternating the colors, over the patches of the previous round, with the points $1\frac{1}{8}$ in from the center.

Round 4 Take 8 patches of fabric A and place them between the patches of the previous round, with their points $1\frac{3}{8}$ in from the center.

Round 5 Take 8 patches of fabric D and place them between the patches of the previous round, with their points $1\frac{5}{8}$ in from the center.

Round 6 Take 8 patches of fabric D and place them between the patches of the previous round, with their points 2 in from the center.

Round 7 Take 16 patches of C and place the first 8 between the patches of the previous round and $2\frac{1}{4}$ in from the center and the remaining 8 in between the first 8 and $2\frac{3}{8}$ in from the center.

Round 8 Take 8 patches of fabric E and place them over the first 8 patches of the previous round, $2\frac{3}{8}$ in from the center.

Round 9 Take 16 patches of fabric B and place them between the patches of the previous round so that their points just reach the position where the patches of rounds 6 and 7 overlap.

Round 10 Take 16 patches of fabric E and place them over the patches of the previous round, with their points 3 in from the center.

The diameter of the patchwork should be $7\frac{3}{4}$ in, plus seam allowances.

6 To make the inner border, first cut a piece of fabric E measuring 11 in square. Set the compass for a radius of $3\frac{3}{4}$ in and, with the point in the center, draw a circle. Draw another circle, with a radius of 5 in, outside it.

7 Machine stitch just outside the inner circle, then cut away the center of the fabric, leaving a $\frac{3}{8}$ in seam allowance inside the line of stitching. Clip at short intervals, almost to the stitching, fold under the seam allowance, and baste.

8 Cut around the outer circle, $\frac{3}{8}$ in outside the marked line.

9 Center the inner border over the patchwork and baste it in place. Machine stitch a scant $\frac{1}{8}$ in from the turned inner edge.

10 For the outer border cut a piece of fabric B measuring 18 in square. Using the compass, draw two concentric circles, one with a radius of $4\frac{7}{8}$ in and one with a radius of 8 in.

11 Prepare the inner edge as described in step 7, then machine stitch around the outer circle.

12 Position the outer border over the inner one so that the turned edge just hides the stitching line. Baste, then machine stitch as in step 9. Baste the border to the backing just inside the outer stitching line.

13 Divide the outer circle into 16 equal segments and machine quilt in overlapping diagonal lines between the inner and outer edges of the outer border (see photograph). Cut around the outer circle, $\frac{1}{2}$ in from the stitching line.

14 From fabric A, cut and piece enough 2 in-wide bias strips (see page 166) to make a strip 50 in long. Cover the filler cord with the bias strip.

15 Pin and baste the cording to the outer border so that the cord lies just inside the stitching line. Join the ends of the cord as shown on page 166.

16 On the remaining piece of fabric A, use the compass to draw 2 half circles, with a radius of $8\frac{1}{2}$ in. Add $\frac{3}{4}$ in seam allowance to the straight sides.
17 Place the two half circles together with right sides facing and raw edges matching. Pin and stitch along the straight edges, taking $\frac{3}{4}$ in seam allowance and leaving $12\frac{1}{2}$ in open in the center.
18 Insert the zipper into the opening. Open the zipper.
19 Place the patchwork and the back piece together with right sides facing. Making sure that the zipper is open, baste all around the edge. Stitch, using the zipper foot and working close to the cord.
20 Turn the pillow cover right side out and insert the pillow form. (If a pillow form of the correct size is not available, make one from two circles of unbleached muslin, 17 in in diameter, stuffed – not too firmly – with fiberfill.)

Blue pillow

1 Using the steel ruler and craft knife, cut a cardboard template 2 in by $3\frac{1}{2}$ in.
2 Use this template to cut the following patches: fabric A, 16 patches; fabric B, 12 patches; fabric C, 12 patches; fabric D, 12 patches.
3 Cut the backing fabric to measure $16\frac{1}{2}$ in square. Using the fabric marking pen, mark it as described for the Peach pillow, step 3.
4 Fold and press each patch as shown in step 2, page 131.
5 Pin and tack the patches to the backing fabric as shown in step 4, page 131, in the following order:
Round 1 As for the Peach pillow, using fabric A.
Round 2 Take 8 patches of fabric A and place 4 of those over the previous round and the rest between them, all $\frac{3}{8}$ in from the center.
Round 3 Take 4 patches of fabric B and place them between those of the previous round, then place 4 patches of fabric D between the first 4, all 1 in from the center.
Round 4 Place 8 patches of fabric B over the patches of the previous round, with their points $1\frac{1}{2}$ in from the center.
Round 5 Take 4 patches of fabric D and place them overlapping the 2 patches of fabric B in rounds 3 and 4, then take 4 patches of fabric A and place them in between the first 4 patches. The points of all the patches should lie $2\frac{1}{4}$ in from the center.
Round 6 Take 8 patches of fabric D and place them over the patches of the previous round, with their points $2\frac{1}{2}$ in from the center.
Round 7 Take 8 patches of fabric C and place them between the patches of the previous round, with their points $2\frac{3}{4}$ in from the center.
　The area of patchwork to be shown measures $8\frac{1}{4}$ in in diameter.
6 Cut a piece of fabric A measuring $16\frac{1}{2}$ in square. Using the compass, draw 2 concentric circles on the fabric, with radii of $4\frac{1}{8}$ in and $7\frac{1}{4}$ in.
7 Finish the inner circle as described for the Peach pillow, step 7.
8 Machine stitch around the outer circle. Position the border over the patchwork so that the design is centered within the border. Baste and machine stitch a scant $\frac{1}{8}$ in from the turned-under edge. Baste the border to the backing just inside the outer stitching line.
9 Cut around the outer circle, $\frac{1}{2}$ in from the stitching line.
10 From fabric A, cut and piece enough 2 in-wide bias strips (see page 166) to make a strip 48 in long. Cover the filler cord with the bias strip.
11 Attach the cording to the pillow cover as described for the Peach pillow.
12 From fabric A, cut the back cover pieces as for the Peach pillow, step 16, but using a radius of $7\frac{1}{4}$ in.
13 Complete the cover as described for the Peach pillow, steps 17 – 20.

Blue pillow
Size
approximately $14\frac{1}{2}$ in in diameter

You will need:
5 different lightweight cotton fabrics, 36 in wide, in the following amounts:

Fabric A (medium blue), $\frac{7}{8}$ yd

Fabric B (blue and white print), $\frac{1}{8}$ yd

Fabric C (small light blue print), $\frac{1}{8}$ yd

Fabric D (small dark blue print), $\frac{1}{8}$ yd

$\frac{1}{2}$ yd of unbleached muslin

48 in of $\frac{3}{8}$ in-diameter filler cord

Round pillow form, 14 in in diameter (or unbleached muslin and fiberfill)

12 in zipper

Cardboard for template

Steel ruler

Craft knife

Compass

Colored pencil or fabric-marking pen

Sewing equipment and threads

SEMINOLE PATCHWORK

Until the early 1900s the Seminole and Miccosukee Indians were living in near-isolation in the swamps of southern Florida. Even so, the sewing machine had already reached them, and they had begun to develop an ingenious – and at the same time basically simple – machine patchwork technique, making decorative bands to attach to ceremonial clothing.

The Indians used brilliant colors, arranging them in many different geometric patterns, formed from pieces much smaller than those generally used in traditional patchwork. This is achieved by cutting narrow strips from a selection of different fabrics, sewing them together, and then cutting the resulting piece into shorter, multicolored strips, which are then staggered and re-joined to form the desired pattern. Although the result may appear complicated, the method is really very quick and can be adapted for some traditional block patchwork designs.

Seminole patchwork can be put to innumerable uses. The colors can be bright and eye-catching or subtle and harmonious. The strips can be cut fairly wide for use on large items such as quilts and wall hangings, but the small size of the patches normally used is often a very useful feature. Unlike traditional patchwork, which developed mainly in conjunction with quilt-making, Seminole patchwork originated as a decoration for clothing and can be used to make strikingly attractive yokes, cuffs, insets, and edgings for shirts and dresses. Because of its small scale, it is especially well suited to children's clothes. It can also be used for accessories such as book covers, bags, mats, belts, and straps.

Fabrics suitable for Seminole patchwork are lightweight, firmly-woven, and fairly crisp, so that the seams can be pressed flat. Lawn is too fine and soft; denim too bulky. All the fabrics used in a piece should be of a similar weight, both for a harmonious texture and to facilitate accuracy when joining strips. Patterned fabrics can be used, but only if the prints are small-scale ones which will not detract from the overall pattern of the patchwork.

The Seminole technique used more fabric than most patchwork because of the numerous seam allowances; and therefore it is not usually possible to use scraps, except for small projects. Ribbons can be used, provided they are at least 1 in wide (for a ½ in-wide strip, after seaming). Satin and moiré ribbons, for example, could be used for an evening bag. Experiment with various fabrics and patterns before embarking on a project. Make several samples, and keep a note of the measurements of the strips used for them.

Measuring and marking equipment Templates are not required for Seminole patchwork, although it is possible to buy transparent strips especially designed for this work in some quilters' shops. Or you can simply use a yardstick to mark long strips and a ruler for short ones and for measuring widths. Plastic and metal rulers are more accurate than wooden ones. A right-angled triangle is useful for making accurate 90° angles and diagonals. Well-sharpened colored pencils in light and dark colors are used to mark the fabrics. To keep the fabric flat and smooth while marking, use strips of masking tape.

1 Marking and cutting To minimize stretching, it is best to cut strips parallel to the selvage, following the lengthwise grain. On small amounts of fabric this is not possible, so cut on the crosswise grain, which is at right angles to the selvage. To find the crosswise grain, either tear the fabric from selvage to selvage or pull out a single thread right across the width. Keeping the fabric flat with masking tape, mark it carefully on the wrong side, using a yardstick or ruler and a colored pencil.

2 Assembling strips It is important to sew the seams as straight as possible; the narrower the strip, the more difficult this will be. Line up the edge of the material with the side of the presser foot to give a $\frac{1}{4}$ in seam allowance and set the machine to about 12 stitches per inch. Join all the strips before pressing the seams, in order to prevent stretching. Press seams open to reduce bulk.

3 Marking the pieces Mark out the pattern on the right side of the joined piece. Straighten the left edge by marking a vertical line, using a well-sharpened colored pencil and a right-angled triangle. Using this as a guideline, measure carefully and mark the beginning and end of each cutting line with a small dot on the outer edges of the piece. Keeping the piece flat with masking tape and moving the ruler as little as possible, join the dots with straight lines and then carefully cut out the multicolored strips. For diagonal lines, use one of the acute angles of the triangle. (This is normally 45°, but it is possible to buy triangles with different angles.)

4 Joining the pieces Lay the pieces out in the correct order and pin them together, with right sides facing, staggering them as desired. Stitch, and then press seams open. When sewing several identical pieces it is quicker to use a continuous line of thread and feed the pieces through, making a long chain of patchwork and leaving the trimming and pressing of seams till later. First stitch the units into pairs, then join the pairs together, and so on, making progressively bigger units until the band is complete.

5 Diagonal ends To straighten the ends of a band formed of strips joined diagonally, cut the band vertically at an appropriate place and then join the two original ends of the band diagonally, as before. In addition to straightening the ends of the band, this will also increase its usable length. If the band includes differing widths or color sequences it is important to make sure that the sloping edges will join up in the correct design sequence.

6 Finishing edges Plain horizontal strips can be used to increase the depth of a finished piece, to finish the edges and to attach the piece to another piece of patchwork or material. Start by trimming off the points of the patchwork to make a straight line. Take the plain strip and pin it to the patchwork, right sides together, and stitch in the usual way. Place the patchwork on top when stitching, so that the seams can be kept flat. Press the seam toward the edging strip.

SEMINOLE PATCHWORK

CANVAS HOLDALL

Bright bands of Seminole patchwork make the pocket of this practical, easy-to-make holdall. Use dressweight cottons for the patchwork and light-weight canvas for the bag.

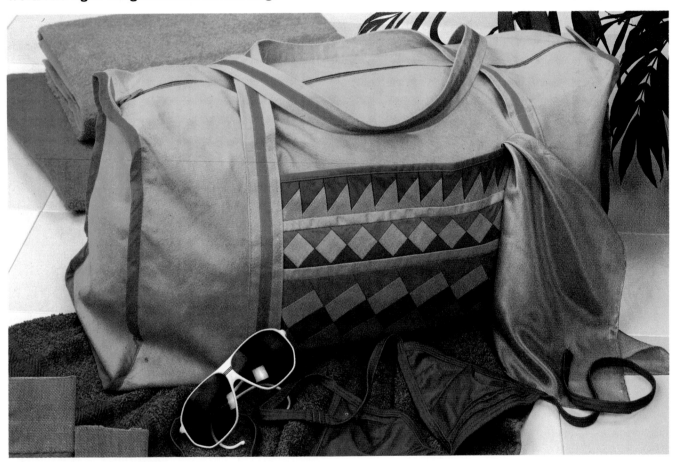

Making the patchwork

1 Cut a strip of blue and a strip of green fabric, each 1½ in wide and 18 in long. Join the strips lengthwise, taking ¼ in seam allowance; then press the seam open.

2 Mark the strip at 2¼ in intervals, using the triangle to make 45° angles. (Hold the strip in place with masking tape.) Cut along the marks.

3 Place 2 pieces side by side, so that the blue strips are aligned at the top corners. Still keeping them aligned, pin and stitch the pieces together with right sides facing (see step 4, page 138), taking ¼ in seam allowance. Press the seam open. Continue joining pieces in the same way. Trim the edges to make a strip 2⅛ in wide and approximately 14 in long.

4 Cut 3 strips, each 18 in long: one each of pink and blue, 1¾ in wide, and one of yellow, 1½ in wide. Join the strips lengthwise with the yellow strips in the middle, as shown on page 140.

Size

approximately 24 in by 13 in

You will need:

4 dressweight cotton fabrics, 36 in wide, in the following amounts:

Pink, $\frac{3}{4}$ yd

Yellow, $\frac{1}{4}$ yd

Blue, $\frac{1}{4}$ yd

Olive green, $\frac{1}{4}$ yd

2$\frac{1}{4}$ yd of lightweight yellow canvas, 36 in wide

22 in separating zipper

Piece of thick cardboard 22$\frac{1}{2}$ in by 8 in for the base

Colored pencils

Ruler

Right-angled triangle

Sewing equipment and threads

Joining the pieces for the middle strip (above) and bottom strip (below)

5 Straighten the left-hand edge and mark the strip vertically at 1$\frac{1}{2}$ in intervals; cut along the marks.

6 Re-join the pieces, staggering them so that the seam joining a pink and yellow strip will be aligned – after seaming – with one joining a yellow and blue strip.

7 Trim the edges to make a strip 2$\frac{1}{8}$ in wide at the seams and approximately 14 in long.

8 Cut 4 strips, each 18 in long: 2 each of pink and green, 2$\frac{1}{4}$ in wide, and 2 each of blue and yellow, 1$\frac{1}{2}$ in wide. Join them lengthwise with the narrow strips in the center, as shown at left.

9 Straighten the left-hand edge and mark the strip vertically at 2$\frac{1}{4}$ in intervals; cut along the marks.

10 Re-join the pieces, staggering them so that adjacent blue and yellow strips will be aligned *after seaming*, as shown.

11 Trim the edges to make a strip 3$\frac{3}{4}$ in wide and approximately 14 in long.

12 Cut 4 strips of fabric, each 1 in by 14 in: one pink, one blue, and 2 yellow. Pin and stitch these to the patchwork strips, following the arrangement shown in the photograph and taking $\frac{1}{4}$ in seam allowance. Press the seams open.

13 Cut a piece of canvas the same size as the patchwork. Place it and the patchwork together, with right sides facing, and pin and stitch $\frac{1}{4}$ in from the top and bottom edges.

14 Turn the pocket right side out. Topstitch along the pink strip, close to the patchwork, to keep the edge flat.

Making the bag

1 Cut the pieces for the bag: one piece 24 in by 39 in for the main section; 2 pieces, each 3$\frac{1}{2}$ in by 55 in, for the straps; and 2 end pieces, each 13 in long, 9 in wide at one end, and 4 in at the other end. Trim these end pieces slightly to round the corners. All pieces include $\frac{3}{8}$ in seam allowance.

2 Turn under and press $\frac{3}{8}$ in on each end of the main piece. Pin and baste one half of the zipper to each folded edge, leaving 1 in margin at top and bottom. Stitch.

3 Turn under and press $\frac{3}{8}$ in on the long edges of both straps. Fold these edges so that they meet in the center of the strap. Press the strap flat.

4 From the remaining pink fabric cut and join enough 1 in wide bias strips (see page 166) to make a strip 115 in long and enough 1$\frac{1}{2}$ in strips to make one 85 in long. Cut each strip in half; turn under and press $\frac{1}{4}$ in on the long edges.

5 Pin and baste the narrower binding strips down the center of each strap, covering the folded canvas edges. Stitch the binding in place, close to the edges, using pink thread in the needle and yellow in the bobbin.

6 Lay the main section on a flat surface, right side up, and place the pocket on top, 4$\frac{3}{8}$ in down from the top edge and the same distance from each side. Pin, baste, and stitch the pocket in place along its lower edge.

7 Turn under and press $\frac{3}{8}$ in on each end of each strap. Position the straps as shown on the diagram, with their ends meeting in the center and their outer edge 4$\frac{3}{4}$ in from the raw edges of the bag. Pin and baste the straps in place, covering the raw edges of the patchwork. Stitch close to the edges of the straps, attaching the front strip first. Take the stitching about 1 in above the top of the pocket and stitch a square shape at that point, for extra strength. Stitch the back strap in the same way.

8 To make a firm base for the bag, cut a piece of canvas 23½ in by 9 in. Turn under and press ⅜ in on the long sides, then on the short sides, Place this piece on the base of the bag, wrong sides facing, and topstitch it in place ⅛ in in from both long sides. (The ends are left open for inserting the cardboard.)

9 To give the bag a finished appearance, make 2 small tongues of fabric to cover the ends of the zipper. Cut 4 pieces of canvas, 2⅜ in square. Trim 2 adjacent corners on each piece (cutting 2 pieces together) to make a rounded shape. Stitch the pieces together, leaving the straight ends open. Trim the seams, turn the tongues right side out, and press.

10 Bring the ends of the bag together and close the zipper. Place one fabric tongue at each end of the zipper; baste and stitch the tongues in place.

11 Fold each end piece in half lengthwise; press to mark the center line. Using the fabric marking pen, mark the stitching line, ⅜ in from the edge on the right side of each piece.

12 Placing wrong sides together, pin and baste the end pieces to the open ends of the bag, easing any fullness at the corners on the end panels, not on the main section.

13 Fold one of the binding strips in half lengthwise; press. Pin and baste it over the raw edges of the bag, trimming any excess and turning under one end to cover the raw edge of the other end. (Place this joining at the bottom of the bag.)

14 Topstitch the binding in place, working through all layers of fabric. (If your machine has trouble coping with this thickness, remove the binding, machine stitch the bag sections together, then apply the binding by hand. Repeat steps 13 and 14 to join and bind the edges at the other end.

15 To complete the bag, turn it wrong side out, insert the piece of cardboard, and turn it right side out again.

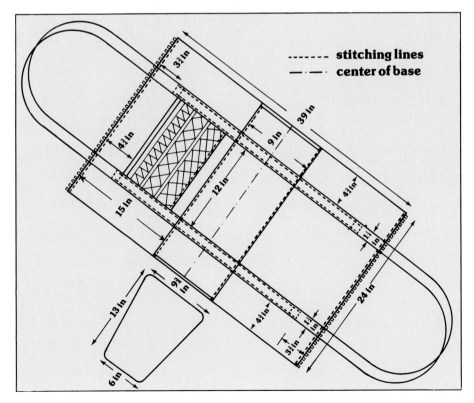

Assembling diagram for the bag (left) and detail of the patchwork (above)

APPLIQUE

Appliqué is one of the most universal forms of needlework. It has been used to decorate the clothing of people as widely scattered as the North American Indians, the Maori tribes of New Zealand, the Tibetans, and the Fon of Dahomey in West Africa. Elaborate forms of appliqué worked in silk and gold were developed in Japan and also in medieval Europe, where appliqué was used on religious vestments and ceremonial banners. In the 18th and 19th centuries, in Britain and North America, appliqué was used in conjunction with patchwork in the making of quilts and other household furnishings. Many of the most popular traditional patchwork blocks incorporate appliqué. "Grandmother's Fan" (see page 104) is an example.

Basically, appliqué consists of cutting a shape from one fabric and sewing it onto another, but within this category are many different techniques, ranging from extremely simple to very complex.

Today, as in the past, appliqué is often used to decorate clothing. An appliqué motif can brighten up and personalize a child's pair of overalls (and perhaps conceal a torn place, thus serving its original function). In more sophisticated forms, appliqué is often used by fashion designers to add a touch of wit or elegance to a garment.

Many artists are also finding appliqué a fascinating medium in which to work. The enormous range of textures available with fabrics – not to mention the threads and stitches used to apply them – provides endless opportunities for creative innovation.

However, you need not be an artist to achieve exciting effects with this craft. All you need is a simple design, some interesting fabrics, and a willingness to experiment.

These projects can be made by adapting the techniques described in the following pages.

APPLIQUE BASICS

Appliqué can be as simple or as complex as you like. It can be worked by hand or by machine and can use all sorts of fabrics and an infinite variety of shapes. The methods used for different forms of appliqué are described in the following pages. Here are some principles that apply to most methods.

Fabrics for appliqué

An enormous range of fabrics can be used for appliqué. The choice in any given case depends on the specific technique being used, how much wear the item will be subjected to, whether or not it is intended to be washable, and, of course, the particular effect desired.

If the object is to be laundered, you should choose appliqué fabrics that are compatible with the background fabric and that are fairly hard-wearing. Cotton and cotton-synthetic blends are the best choice. Generally, the fabrics should be of a similar weight, although this does not rule out an interesting variation in texture. A lightweight corduroy might combine well with poplin or denim, for example.

If the raw edges of the motif are to be turned under, it is important to choose a fabric that will take a crease well. Those that stretch and those that fray easily are best avoided. However, a fabric that frays or is too flimsy to be used as it is can be reinforced with iron-on interfacing. First trace the motif from interfacing (adhesive side up) and cut it out. Iron it to the wrong side of the fabric, and then cut out the motif. Apply the shape either with machine zigzag stitch or with hand embroidery, covering the raw edges.

You can exploit the textures of fabrics in interesting ways: use black velvet for a cat, for example, or shantung for the bark of a tree. Prints, too, can be exploited in this way: a small floral print might suggest a garden.

Designing

Ideas can come from almost any source: a painting, a piece of china, wallpaper, the illustrations in children's books, photographs. Make a collection of clippings from magazines and postcards from art museums.

There are various ways of designing a piece of appliqué. For a simple piece of work involving only one or a few shapes, the best method may be to trace the motifs, enlarge them if necessary (see page 167), and then move them around on a sheet of paper the size of the background until you achieve a pleasing arrangement. For a more complex design, draw the design completely, using pencil or pen, color it with paints, crayons, or colored pencils, and then enlarge it. If you are tracing it from a picture, simplify the shapes so that they will be easy to cut out and apply — you can add details with embroidery stitches later.

If you are happier working with scissors than with pen or pencil, try cutting paper shapes, using paper in the colors you are using for the appliqué. Very pretty shapes can be produced by folding the paper and then cutting (see Hawaiian Quilting, page 157); or you can simply draw a circle on colored paper, using a plate or compass, then cut it into irregular pieces. Move the pieces around on a sheet of paper until you obtain a pleasing design. Glue them in place and use this as the master pattern for the appliqué.

SIMPLE HAND APPLIQUE

For a simple introduction to hand appliqué, use felt, which is easy to cut and sew and comes in bright colors. Or, if you prefer, use a closely woven cotton fabric and back it with iron-on interfacing.

In this type of appliqué the stitches are worked over the fabric edges. You can make them inconspicuous by using ordinary sewing thread in matching colors, or you can use an embroidery thread, such as pearl cotton or several strands of embroidery floss, in colors to match or contrast with the fabrics, and so make a feature of the stitching.

For enlarging and transferring the design, you will need graph paper, tracing paper, thin cardboard, and scissors for cutting paper.

1 Tracing the design First enlarge the design as required (see page 167), then trace it on a large sheet of tracing paper. This tracing will be used to check that the appliqué shapes have been positioned correctly on the background fabric. Pencil a number on each outlined shape on the tracing.

2 Tracing the shapes Take another sheet of tracing paper and trace each of the numbered shapes separately. Cut them out and number them, using the same numbers as on the design tracing. Make sure that each tracing matches the original design. Where shapes overlap, you can either cut away the underlying shape or simply overlap the fabrics, if the amount is small. Details such as narrow stems can be cut freehand, worked in embroidery, or made from ribbon or trimmings.

3 Cutting the fabric Use the tracings to cut templates from thin cardboard. Then lay the templates on the wrong side of the fabric with the numbered sides facing down. Draw around each shape and cut it out carefully. Lightly pencil the number of the template on the wrong side of the fabric.

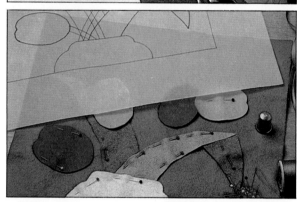

4 Positioning the shapes Lay the fabric shapes which you have cut out on the background material in their approximate positions, with the numbered sides down. Place the design tracing on top of them and move the shapes around underneath it until they are correctly positioned. Pin each shape in place, and baste around the edges.

5 Sewing the shapes Hand appliqué work can be sewn to the background fabric in many ways. The simple overcast stitch (right) is one of the quickest and easiest. Running stitch (center) and backstitch (left) are equally suitable. When sewing the shapes to the background, first sew on those which pass underneath other pieces. Where two shapes touch, make sure that there is no visible gap by sewing one of the edges to the other.

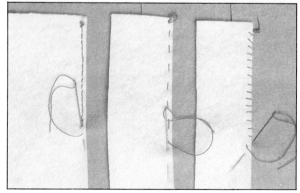

TULIP MOTIF PLACEMATS

Easy-to-handle felt is used for the bright tulip shapes appliquéd onto these placemats. Make several, varying the color combination on each.

Working the appliqué

1 Enlarge the design given on page 148 to fit within a 10 in by 7 in rectangle.
2 Trace the enlarged design and number the shapes. Make another tracing of the individual appliqué shapes (see step 2, page 146), and number these shapes as before.
3 Use the traced shapes to make templates from thin cardboard.

Size

13 in by 10 in

You will need:

(for one placemat)

Piece of blue felt 13 in by 10 in

Piece of patterned fabric 16 in by 13 in

Scraps of red, pink, yellow, light green, and dark green felt

⅜ yd of ⅜ in-wide green satin ribbon

1½ yd of ½ in-wide single fold red bias tape

Graph paper

Tracing paper

Thin cardboard

Tailor's chalk or colored pencil

Silicon spray

Sewing equipment and threads

4 Cut each shape from the appropriately colored felt as follows: template 1, red; template 2, dark green; template 3, pink; template 4, red; template 5, pink; template 6, light green; template 7, dark green; template 8, yellow. Number the shapes on the wrong side (check each against the enlarged design to ascertain which is the wrong side). For the stems, cut 4 pieces of ribbon: 6 in, 3 in, 1½ in, and 1 in long.

5 Using tailor's chalk or colored pencil and a ruler, mark off a 1½ in border on all edges of the piece of blue felt.

6 Pin the appliqué shapes to the blue background, inside the border, referring to the master tracing to check that the positioning is correct.

7 Using matching thread and either running stitch, backstitch, or overcasting, sew each shape in place. When sewing, make sure that pieces which lie under other pieces are sewn down first. For example, sew piece 4 before attaching piece 5. Where two shapes touch – for example, 3 and 2, or 6 and 7 – make sure that there is no visible gap by sewing one edge to the other. Three of the ribbon stems must tuck under the edge of piece 8, so leave that edge unstitched for the moment.

8 Sew on the ribbon stems: first turn under the end that joins the flower and sew it in place, using small stitches. Then pin the rest of the ribbon to the background, tucking the other end under the bowl or leaf, as appropriate, and sew it in place. Sew down the remaining free edges. Press the work.

Finishing the mat

1 On the patterned fabric turn 1½ in to the wrong side on the top and bottom edges; press. Repeat on the side edges.

2 Place the appliquéd piece in the center of the patterned fabric, with the turned edges enclosing it. Pin and baste around the edges. Slipstitch the openings at the four corners.

3 Cut 4 strips of bias tape; 2 of them 14 in long and 2 of them 11 in long. Pin and baste them over the raw edges of the patterned fabric, tucking under ½ in at each end. Topstitch close to all edges.

4 Protect the mat with silicon spray (felt is not washable).

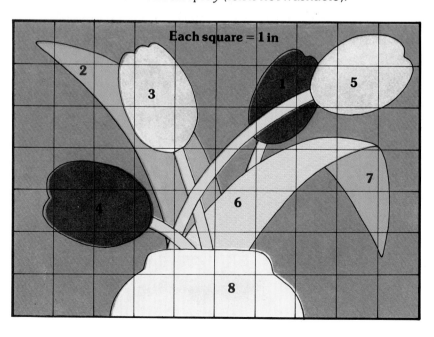

Pattern for the appliqué

MACHINE APPLIQUE

People tend to think that hand crafts are superior to machine crafts, assuming that there is a particular virtue in doing something laboriously by hand instead of quickly by machine, but machine-made items can have just as much charm and individuality as those made by hand. In the case of appliqué, machine work has certain advantages that make it preferable to the hand-sewn type in many instances.

One of these advantages is the greater range of fabrics that can be used. Many synthetics and heavy fabrics, such as velvets and brocades, that are difficult to sew by hand can easily be applied by machine. Fabrics that fray easily present little problem for machine appliqué, since the raw edges are thoroughly covered.

Machine appliqué is particularly suitable for articles that will be subjected to hard wear and that will be machine washed, because machine stitching is far firmer and stronger than hand sewing. And because it is so strong, machine appliqué is ideal for patching a garment that is torn or showing signs of wear.

Fabrics suitable for machine appliqué can include almost anything, depending on whether or not the finished item must be washed. Beginners may prefer to start with the firm, dressweight cottons that are so suitable for hand appliqué, as these are easiest to keep in place. However, it is well worthwhile experimenting with other materials, such as corduroy, tweed, lace, and leather. Iron-on interfacing can be used to back fabrics that fray easily.

Threads Polyester-cotton is suitable for most stitching. Buy the largest spools you can find (machine appliqué uses up a lot of thread), if possible getting them in boxes from dressmakers' suppliers. For special effects, use silk or metallic thread in the needle (ordinary thread, in a matching color, in the bobbin). A thread that contrasts with the fabric can often be used to good effect.

Machine This must be equipped with a zigzag stitch, and must be in good working order. Have a good supply of needles on hand, including a variety of sizes and types suitable for different fabrics. Never use a needle that has become blunt or rusty.

Other materials needed include graph paper, tracing paper, and thin cardboard for templates.

1 Preparation Draw the design and make templates as for hand appliqué, but remember that no seam allowance is needed, since the edges will be covered. A problem that many people have with machine appliqué is avoiding puckers and wrinkles, and preparation is very important here. Baste the pieces firmly in place about $\frac{1}{4}$ in from the edge (in some cases it may be better to baste so close to the edge that the basting will be covered by the zigzag stitch). Press the work well to make sure that it is completely flat.

2 Stitching Stitch with the machine set at a close zigzag stitch, keeping the work flat with your hands. Some people find that it is easier to prevent wrinkles if the fabric is held in an embroidery hoop. (Mount the fabric in the hoop wrong side up, so that the right side will be up on the machine. Remove the presser foot to slide the hoop onto the machine.) The closeness of the stitches remains the same throughout, but the width may need to be reduced at sharp corners. Begin and end sewing with a few reverse stitches.

3 Order of work The fabric may tend to move a little during stitching so that a small pucker of material is left at the end (although good basting will help to prevent this problem). It is therefore best to begin by stitching all the pieces which are partly covered by other shapes, so that any small pleats of fabric can be eased under the top piece before that is sewn down.

4 Zigzag effects The zigzag width can be varied to some extent, but do not try to sew with the stitches very close together, as this will tend to clog the machine. One way to achieve a thicker-looking stitch is to stitch twice, making the stitches of the top row slightly wider than the first. In this way, the first row acts as a base for the second, giving it a slightly raised appearance similar to the effects that can be produced with industrial machines. When stitching points, you may need to narrow the stitch.

5 Decoration You need not confine the stitching to the edge of the fabric. Use the machine to draw details and features in the center, or at the edges of an applied piece, preferably in a contrasting color. If the machine is equipped with a range of embroidery stitches you can use them in various ways — for example, to embroider the center of a flower.

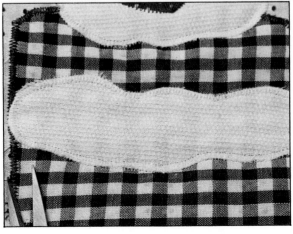

6 Finishing When all the pieces have been applied, finish off the work. Trim all the loose ends of thread and go around each piece very carefully with sharp embroidery scissors, snipping off any raw edges or bits of thread that project beyond the stitching line. Remove all visible basting threads and finish by pressing the work, easing out any small wrinkles.

MACHINE-APPLIQUED APRONS

Mouth-watering strawberry shortcakes give a touch of culinary class to these practical bib-top aprons.

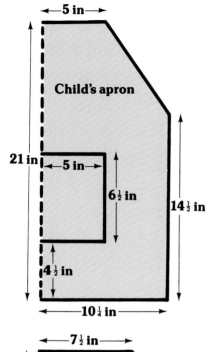

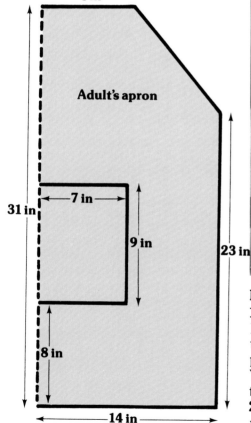

Measurement diagram for the aprons

Making the aprons

1 Cut the two pieces for each apron, following the measurements at left. Fold the fabric in half lengthwise to cut the main piece for the adult size, then fold it lengthwise again, just wide enough to cut the child's size; cut the pockets from the remaining fabric, noting that they, too, are cut on the fold. You can either mark the shapes directly on the fabric, using a yardstick and tailor's chalk, or make paper patterns first.

2 On the main pattern piece, turn under ¼ in on all edges and topstitch it in place. Then turn under another ½ in on the top and bottom edges; topstitch. Repeat on the side edges, up to the sloping edges. Turn under 1¼ in on the sloping edges and topstitch 1⅛ in from the fold to make a casing for the tape.

3 Finish the raw edges of the pockets with zigzag stitch. Turn under $\frac{3}{8}$ in on one long edge (the top edge) and topstitch. Turn under $\frac{1}{4}$ in on the other three edges, mitering the corners (see page 166), and baste. Baste the pocket to the front of the apron, positioning it as shown on the measurement diagram. Topstitch it in place, close to the edge.

Working the appliqué

It is a good idea to start with the child's version, since this is slightly simpler than the adult's.

1 Enlarge the appliqué design as indicated (see page 167). Trace the shapes for the appliqué. Number the shapes on the design and the individual shapes. (Note: because the strawberries and leaves are so small, it might be easier to cut these – and the small blobs of cream – freehand from the cloth, without bothering to make tracings and templates.)

2 Use the individual tracings to make templates from thin cardboard. Number these also.

3 Cut the shapes from the appropriate fabrics. Where a piece will be over-lapped by another piece, cut a little generously so that no space will show between them.

4 Pin, baste, and stitch the pieces, one at a time, to the apron, as described in steps 1-3, page 150, pressing the work before stitching to prevent wrinkles, and applying the pieces in the following order: plate, cake, cream, strawberries, and leaves. When stitching the leaves, you may need to narrow the stitch at the points.

5 Finish the work by snipping any loose threads and then pressing. Thread the woven tape through the casings at the sides.

Size

adult's apron: $29\frac{1}{2}$ in long
child's apron: $19\frac{1}{2}$ in long

You will need:

(for both aprons)

$1\frac{1}{2}$ yd of 36 in-wide cotton drill, or other heavy cotton

4 yd of 1 in-wide white woven tape

Scraps of medium-weight cotton fabrics in red, green, white, and beige

Paper for apron patterns, or yardstick and tailor's chalk

Graph paper

Tracing paper

Thin cardboard

Colored pencil or fabric-marking pen

Sewing equipment and threads

Appliqué patterns

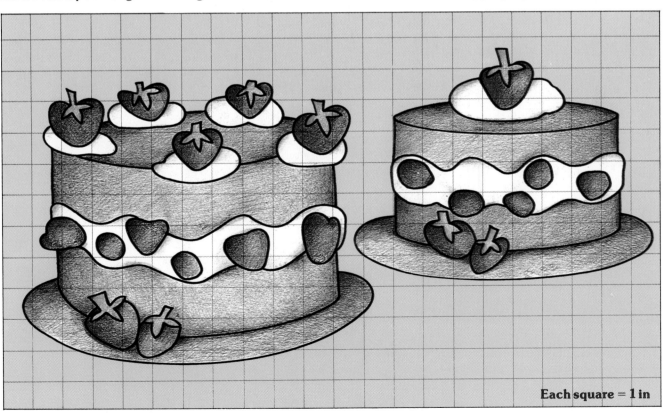

Each square = 1 in

HAWAIIAN QUILTING

This attractive form of appliqué dates from the early 19th century, when American missionaries began to arrive in the Hawaiian Islands. Along with them the missionaries brought beautiful quilts, which the women had made on the long ocean voyages. Their knowledge of sewing was first put to work on the project of getting the Hawaiians to wear western-style clothes, but the quilts and the techniques used in their construction were to stimulate an original Hawaiian form of needlework.

The most popular story told to explain the origin of Hawaiian quilting explains how a woman placed a large piece of fabric on the ground to dry. The shadow from the leaves of a nearby tree etched their design across the solid-colored fabric, and, seeing them, the woman decided to appliqué their shapes onto the fabric.

In the beginning the designs were jealously guarded. Quilts were never displayed, for fear that the design would be copied, and a person who stole a design would be ostracized by other quilters. Gradually, however, the art of making Hawaiian quilts became less popular, and there was some concern that it might die out completely. As a result, some of the older women began teaching tourists their secrets, and now women all over the world are making Hawaiian quilts.

The main difference between Hawaiian quilting and other forms of appliqué is that, in general, only two pieces of fabric are used. The top piece is folded and cut like a paper snowflake and then appliquéd onto the background fabric.

The quilting lines that complement and echo the motif are very intricate. The lines of stitching are made immediately outside the design and then at intervals of about $\frac{1}{2}$ in to the edge of the quilt or pillow cover. This is called "wave" quilting. The central motif is also quilted.

Designing Hawaiian appliqué patterns are essentially personal expressions. It is not always easy to find designs to copy, but it is, on the other hand, very easy to create your own. Experiment by folding a square piece of paper in the same way the fabric is folded in step 1, page 155. Draw a line on the

paper, similar to the patterns for torch ginger and breadfruit given on page 159, then cut along the line to make a folded paper pattern like those sometimes made by children. When you have found a pattern you like, cut out one segment of it (one-eighth of the whole) to use as the pattern for cutting the fabric. If it needs enlarging, trace around it, then scale it up using the method described on page 167.

For the appliqué you can use either the positive or the negative pattern produced by your paper cutting: compare the two designs shown on page 159. Use strong, solid colors for this work to get a good contrast between appliqué and background and to suggest the flowers and foliage of the Hawaiian Islands.

Fabrics Firmly-woven dressweight cotton is the best choice for the appliqué motif. The background fabric can be a cotton-synthetic blend, but should be easy to quilt by hand. All fabrics should be prewashed before use to get rid of any finish in them. Check for colorfastness by soaking each piece in hand-hot water in a white basin.

Great care must be taken when pressing to make sure that the grain lines cross at right angles. Pull the fabric if necessary to straighten it.

The backing fabric used underneath the batting should be lawn, or a similar lightweight fabric. The batting itself should be lightweight, for ease in hand quilting.

Threads Use ordinary cotton-polyester thread for the appliqué, quilting thread for the lines of quilting.

Sewing equipment You will need very good quality, sharp dressmaking scissors which will cut through 8 thicknesses of fabric without difficulty, small embroidery scissors, and a betweens needle, size 8 or 9. A large quilting hoop is useful for working the quilting.

Materials for transferring the design For patterns you will need ordinary drawing paper, tracing paper, possibly graph paper, scissors for cutting paper, a pen or pencil suitable for marking fabric, and materials for transferring quilting lines. If you are using the pricking method (see page 12), these will include pounce or talcum powder and a small piece of felt.

1 Pressing From the two fabrics (background and appliqué) cut squares the size of the finished work plus seam allowance — or slightly larger than the quilting hoop. Make sure that the grain runs straight on both pieces. Fold each in half, then in half again, forming a square, and then diagonally, as shown, pressing carefully after each fold.

2 Marking and cutting Mark the straight grain and bias grain on the pattern (long arrow and two short arrows, respectively). Pin the pattern to the folded appliqué fabric, through all 8 thicknesses. Mark around the pattern. Remove the pins and check that they have not caused any distortion of the outline. Remove the pattern, pin the fabric layers together again, and cut around the lines with very sharp scissors.

3 Positioning the design Unfold the background fabric and place it right side up on a flat surface. Carefully unfold the motif and place it on the background fabric. Pin the centers together, then continue pinning, working from the center outward to all parts of the design and matching the fold lines exactly. Baste around the shape, a scant $\frac{3}{8}$ in from the edge.

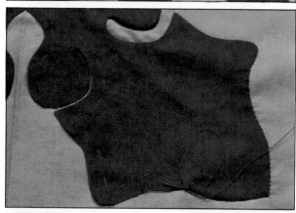

4 Sewing Using thread to match the appliqué motif and beginning at the center, slipstitch the motif in place, turning under $\frac{1}{8}$ in with the point of the needle as you go. Make several stitches at sharp corners to prevent fraying. When sewing points, work as far as the place at which the finished point will end, then turn under the point and continue along the other side.

5 Quilting Transfer the quilting lines by the chosen method. Pin and baste the appliquéd piece, batting, and backing fabric together as described in steps 2 and 3, page 13. More lines of basting will be necessary if a frame is not being used. Hand-quilt around the motif using a betweens needle, quilting thread, and small running stitches (see steps 5-8, page 14). Then quilt the motif, still working in parallel lines placed about $\frac{1}{2}$ in apart.

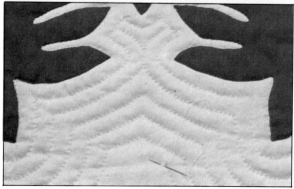

HAWAIIAN-QUILTED PILLOWS

Warm colors, reminiscent of the tropics, are used for these attractive pillow covers, appliquéd with breadfruit and torch ginger motifs. (Note that the green breadfruit leaves fan inward from the edges, whereas the gold torch ginger radiates from the center of the pillow.) The lines of the motifs are echoed by lines of hand quilting — called "wave" quilting — which give a rich texture to the work.

Size
approximately 18 in square

You will need:
(for each pillow)

¾ yd of 48 in-wide firmly-woven cotton fabric in each of two contrasting colors (the back of the cover can be made from the appliqué fabric or background fabric)

Piece of lightweight polyester batting, 24 in square

Piece of backing fabric, such as lawn, 24 in square

Quilting thread to match the fabrics

16 in zipper to match the fabric chosen for the back

18 in square pillow form

Tracing paper

Graph paper

Small piece of felt

Talcum powder

Fabric-marking pen or pencil

Sewing equipment and threads

Appliqué and quilting

1 Enlarge the design on page 159 as indicated. Trace the enlarged drawing, including the quilting lines, on a folded piece of tracing paper, placing the fold on the diagonal line, so that you have one quarter of the design. Make another tracing of the appliqué motif on a single thickness of paper.

2 Cut the fabric for the pillow top and for the appliqué in half crosswise. Put one half of each aside. Trim the other pieces to measure 24 in square; fold and press them as described in step 1, page 155

3 Place the appliqué pattern on the folded piece of appropriate fabric and pin it carefully in place, as shown in step 2, page 156. Mark around the edges with the pencil. Remove the pattern, then replace the pins. Cut around the marked outline with sharp scissors.

4 Unfold the top fabric and place it right side up on a flat surface. Open out the appliqué motif and place it right side up on the background fabric. Pin it in place, matching the fold lines and working from the center outward.

5 Baste the motif to the background fabric, a scant ⅜ in from the edges.

6 Using matching thread and a betweens needle, slipstitch the motif in place. Take tiny stitches and use the needle to turn under the fabric.

7 When the appliqué is complete, press the work.

8 On the tracing of one-quarter of the design, prick holes along the quilting lines with a needle, placing the holes about ⅜ in apart (see page 12).

9 Secure the pillow top to a flat surface with masking tape and place the tracing on one corner, so that the rough side, caused by the pricking, is upward. Transfer the design to the fabric as shown on page 12, using the felt and powder and the fabric-marking pen. Repeat the marking process on the remaining three corners of the work.

10 Assemble the three layers – appliqué top, batting, and backing fabric – and pin and baste them together along the center lines. Mount them in the quilting hoop. (If you are not using a hoop, add more lines of basting.)

11 Using a betweens needle and matching quilting thread, work fine running stitches along the quilting lines.

12 Remove the work from the hoop and trim it evenly to measure 18 in square. Machine stitch around all sides, ¼ in from the edge.

Assembling the cover

The back can be made from either of the two fabrics.

1 Cut 2 pieces of fabric for the back, each measuring 18 in by 10 in. Place them together, with right sides facing, and, taking 1 in seam allowance, stitch along one long side for ¾ in at each end, leaving a 16½ in gap in the middle.

2 Insert the zipper into the opening.

3 With the zipper open, place the front and back of the cover together, right sides facing. Pin, baste, and stitch around the sides, ½ in from the edge.

4 From the fabric selected for the binding, cut 4 strips, each 2½ in wide: 2 measuring 18 in long and 2 measuring 21 in.

5 Take one of the shorter strips and place it right side down along one edge of the front of the cover so that the raw edge of the strips is even with the seamed edge of the cover. Pin and baste it in place, then stitch ½ in from the edge. Trim the excess fabric at the ends, and press the strip away from the pillow. Repeat to join the other shorter strip to the opposite edge.

6 Repeat step 5 to join the longer strips to the remaining sides of the pillow and to the ends of the other strips, trimming and pressing as before.

7 Turn under and press ½ in on the edge of the binding attached in step 5

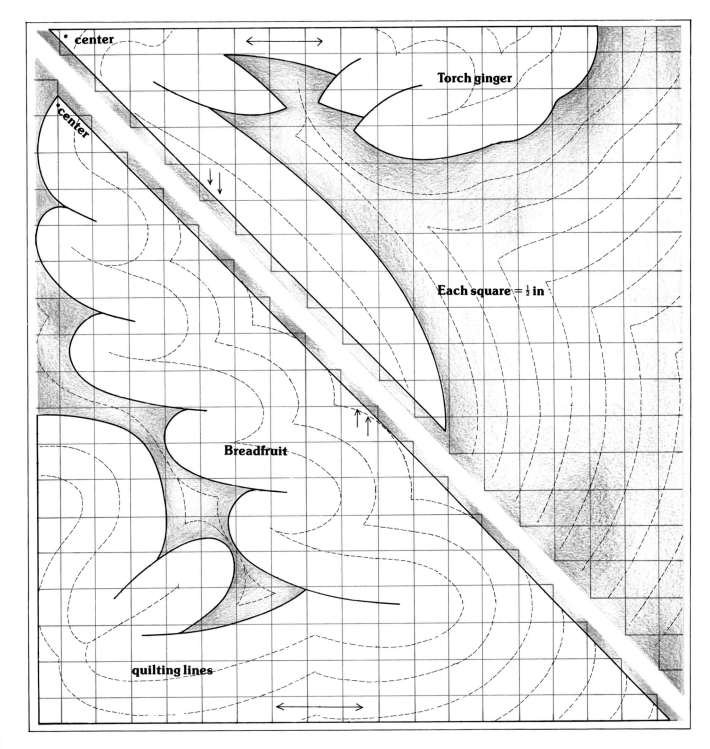

center

Torch ginger

center

Each square = $\frac{1}{2}$ in

Breadfruit

quilting lines

(and the ends of the longer strips). Turn these edges over to the back of the pillow (first trimming away excess fabric at the corners), and baste and slip-stitch them over the line of machine stitching.

8 Repeat step 7 to finish the longer strips of binding. Take care to keep the binding an even width and to make sure that the corners are square. Slip-stitch the remaining gaps at the corners. Insert the pillow form.

Patterns for the appliqué

STAINED GLASS APPLIQUE

Appliqué made to resemble stained glass is a very recent adaptation of the craft. The technique is not difficult. It consists essentially of basting the shapes onto the background fabric and then covering their edges with black bias binding, which is then stitched in place. The colors used are jewel tones, to simulate the appearance of real stained glass. The binding suggests the leading used to join pieces of glass, which not only follows the outlines of the shapes but also cuts across the background forming patterns of its own. Although basically simple, the method requires some patience, since both edges of the binding tape must be sewn by hand, using slipstitch.

Stained glass appliqué can be used for various projects. It lends itself most naturally to window shades and screens placed over windows, where the light will make the colors glow. But it is also possible to use it for strikingly beautiful quilts and bedspreads or to embellish clothing. A fire screen worked in stained glass appliqué would make a dramatic accessory for the living room.

Ideas for stained glass appliqué can be found in real stained glass windows; a detail from a large window might be used. Or you might adapt a design from some boldly printed fabric or wallpaper. It is very important, if the correct effect is to be achieved, to make sure that all the black "lead" lines connect up, just as in real stained glass, and that none of them are left with unsupported ends jutting out into colored areas.

Fabrics of different textures and weaves may be used for stained glass appliqué, but cotton and cotton-polyester blends are easiest to work with. A firm, closely woven white or neutral fabric should be used for the background. Solid colors are generally used for the appliquéd pieces, although some small prints might effectively suggest the bubbles, ripples, or flecks found in stained glass. Varying shades of the same color can be combined successfully; the black tape will emphasize the differences in tone.

The binding must be cut from fabric, preferably cotton: ready-made bias binding is not suitable, since it is too loosely woven and cannot be washed before it is used.

Sewing equipment You will need sharp dressmaking scissors, embroidery scissors, a thimble, and a betweens needle, size 8 or 9.

Materials for transferring You will need several large sheets of paper, graph paper, tracing paper or other translucent paper for the templates, crayons or colored pencils, water colors (optional), a black felt-tip pen, and some masking tape.

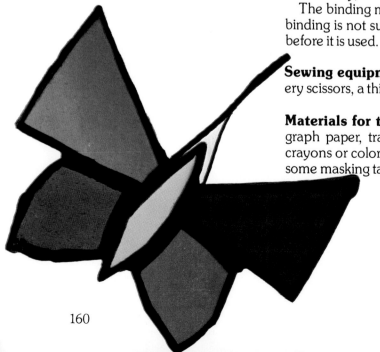

1 Designing Start by making a small-scale version of the design and trying out various color combinations, using crayons or water colors. (First marking the paper into squares will help when enlarging the design.) Outline the shapes with black felt-tip pen to suggest the leading, taking some of the lines across large areas of background as shown. When you are satisfied with the design, enlarge it to the desired size (see page 167).

2 Transferring the design Start by placing the paper design on a flat surface and securing it with masking tape. Place the background fabric over the design and tape it in place. Use a well-sharpened pencil to draw in the design lines. If the lines are not visible through the fabric, go over them with felt-tip pen.

3 Making templates All the pieces that are to be applied should be numbered on the design, and if the design is complicated it may also help to mark in the colors. Trace each shape separately. (There is no need to trace the shapes on the background, the leading lines, or the border strips, if any.) Number and color the templates as shown, and group them according to color.

4 Cutting out Pin the templates to the fabrics and cut out the pieces carefully. If the pieces are very small, it may be better to place the template on the fabric and draw around it, then cut along the drawn line. (Grainlines are not important in this kind of appliqué.) Position the pieces on the background fabric, butting the edges as shown. Pin and baste them in place.

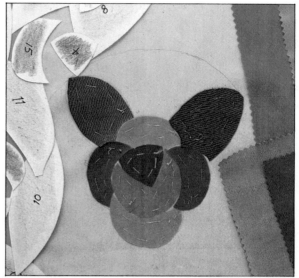

5 Making the tape Mark and cut bias strips (see page 166) twice the desired finished width: those for the window shade on page 163 are cut ¾ in wide. Turn under and press both edges so that they almost meet in the center. The strips will be of various lengths; there is no need to join them, since many different lengths will be needed.

6 Sewing Place the bias tape along the edges of the applied pieces so that half of it lies on one piece and half on another. Pin it in place, covering a small section at a time. Where one strip runs into another, tuck the end under the continuing piece. Slipstitch the tape in place, always working first on the inner edge of a curve, then sewing the outer edge.

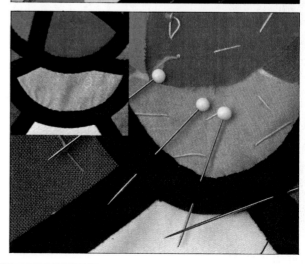

FLORAL WINDOW SHADE

The bright colors of this stained glass appliqué window shade cast a warm glow into a room or hallway.

Size

20 in by 50 in (picture)
20 in by 54½ in (complete shade)

You will need:

2⅜ yd of 36 in-wide black cotton fabric

1½ yd of medium-weight cream-colored fabric, any width

⅜ yd of red fabric, 36 in wide, for the borders and some appliqué pieces

Scraps of blue, yellow, pink, lilac, purple, and 3 shades of green fabric for the appliqué

⅛ yd of 36 in-wide heavy, iron-on interfacing, or fabric stiffening spray

Window shade kit

¾ in-wide wooden batten, 19 in long

Tacks or staples for fastening shade to roller

Graph paper

Black felt-tip pen

Paper (e.g. tracing paper) for templates

Sewing equipment and threads

Working the appliqué

1 Enlarge the design on page 165 as indicated (see page 167) so that it measures 20 in by 50 in. (To make the shade a different size, make the grid squares smaller or larger, as desired.) Darken the lines with felt-tip pen to make them visible through the background fabric.

2 If the shade is to be washable, first wash and iron all the fabrics before marking and cutting them.

3 Cut a 12 in-wide strip of black fabric from the width of the fabric. Set this aside. Cut the remaining fabric in half widthwise to make 2 pieces approximately 36 in square. Fold each piece in half diagonally and press the fold to mark the bias grain.

4 On one piece mark a line 2 in to each side of the fold, parallel to it. Cut along the lines to make 2 bias strips, each 2 in wide. Trim the ends at right angles so that the strips are 49½ in long. Prepare each strip by first folding in the side edges, then folding the strip in half, so that it is about ½ in wide. These strips will be used to bind the side edges.

5 From the same piece of fabric, cut bias strips to go around the inner edges of the red border: cut 2 strips 49¼ in long and 2 strips 16 in long, all 1¼ in wide. Fold and press the strips as described in step 5, page 162, so that the side edges meet in the center and the strips measure about ⅝ in wide.

6 Cut the rest of the black fabric (apart from the 12 in strip) into more bias strips, cutting them ¾ in wide. Fold and press the strips as in step 5, above. Since this tape is used only in short lengths, there is no need to piece strips together.

7 Cut a piece of cream fabric 23 in by 53½ in for the background. Fold it in half lengthwise and press it lightly. On the paper pattern mark the vertical center with a felt-tip pen. Mark the center of the fabric, with pencil, at top and bottom edges. Place the fabric over the pattern, aligning the center lines, and secure them with masking tape. Copy the design onto the background fabric as described in step 2, page 161.

8 Make paper templates for the applied pieces, as shown in step 3, page 161. Label the templates and cut each in the appropriate fabric. Do not cut templates for the red border.

9 Pin and baste each piece to the background fabric, referring to the original pattern and matching numbers.

10 When all the pieces have been basted in place, begin sewing on the bias tape, following the lines of the design and covering the raw edges of the applied shapes. It is important to plan ahead and give some thought to the order of sewing. All tape ends should be concealed under other strips, so apply the underlying pieces first. Hold the tape in position with the left hand (if you are right-handed), and remember on curved sections to pin and sew the inner curve first. Use a small slipstitch for sewing on the tape. (Baste it in place first, if you prefer.) Sew on all the narrow tape except for that covering the tips of the leaves that extend into the red border.

11 For the border, cut 2 in-wide strips of red fabric. These can be of various lengths, since they will be crossed at intervals by pieces of narrow binding.

12 Pin and baste the border pieces in place (cut away small sections where there are projecting leaves).

13 Sew on the short strips of bias tape to make the "lead lines" across the border. Then sew on the long strips of binding to cover the inner edges. Finally, sew on the tape covering the edges of the projecting leaves.

14 Cut enough ¾ in-wide strips of iron-on interfacing to cover the side edges of the shade. Turn the shade wrong side up and apply the interfacing so that one half lies over the red border and the other half over the background fabric. This will stiffen the edges of the shade. (Alternatively, you can spray the shade with stiffening.)

Finishing the shade
1 Cut away the excess background fabric (including the interfacing) along both sides and at the bottom, leaving it intact at the top.
2 Pin and sew the folded binding over the side edges of the shade, using slipstitch. Sew the back edge first, then the top edge.
3 From the remaining 12 in strip of black fabric cut a piece 7 in by 21 in. Turn under and press $\frac{1}{2}$ in on both short edges, then fold the piece in half lengthwise, wrong sides facing, so that it measures $3\frac{1}{2}$ in by 20 in. Press the fold.
4 Slipstitch the short folded edges together.
5 Place the folded strip on the wrong side of the lower edge of the shade, with raw edges matching. Pin and stitch, by machine or by hand, through all layers, taking $\frac{3}{8}$ in seam allowance. Press the seam allowances toward the black strip.
6 Bring the folded edge of the strip to the right side of the shade and pin it over the first stitching line. Slipstitch it in place, thus forming a pocket for the batten.
7 Cut another piece of black fabric 4 in by 21 in. Place it along the upper edge of the shade, with right sides facing and raw edges matching and 1 in of the border strip extending on each side. Stitch, taking $\frac{3}{8}$ in seam allowance. Press the seam allowance toward the strip.
8 Trim the background fabric so that it extends 3 in above the stitching line. Press the side edges of the border over the background fabric, then press the top edge over it. Turn under the raw edges and slipstitch them in place.
9 Attach the shade to the roller, following the manufacturer's instructions. Insert the batten in the pocket.

Pattern for the appliqué

Each square = 2 in

BASIC SKILLS

CUTTING ON THE GRAIN
Instructions often tell you to cut fabric on the "lengthwise grain" or the "crosswise grain." The lengthwise grain is that running parallel to the selvage (the firmly-woven edge of the fabric); the crosswise grain is that running at a 90° angle to the selvage.

"Bias" refers to a diagonal direction, relative to the selvage. The "true bias," which runs at a 45° angle to the selvage, has the most stretch. This should be used for cutting bias strips, to be used as binding or for cording.

BIAS STRIPS

To find the true bias fold the fabric diagonally as shown; press the fold. Using a yardstick and tailor's chalk or marking pen, rule lines parallel to the fold, the specified distance apart. Cut them out.

To join strips to make up the necessary length, place them together, right sides facing, at a 90° angle. Stitch them together as shown and press the seam open.

To make bias binding for edges, fold $\frac{1}{4}$ in – $\frac{3}{8}$ in on one long edge to the wrong side; press. Repeat on the other long edge. (You can buy a gadget that folds both edges simultaneously as you press.)

MAKING AND APPLYING CORDING

1 For cording, cut bias strips twice the seam allowance plus the circumference of the filler cord. Fold the bias strip over the cord as shown and stitch close to it using a zipper foot.

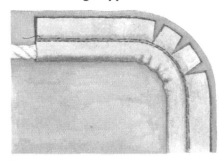

2 To apply the cord to the edge, pin and baste it to the right side of the fabric, clipping the seam allowance where necessary.

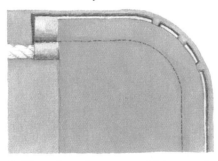

3 Place the other piece of fabric, right side down, on top of the first, enclosing the cording. Baste and stitch, using a zipper foot, as close as possible to the cording, to cover the first stitching.

JOINING ENDS OF CORDING
Where cording goes around the entire edge of an object, such as a pillow, the ends must be joined neatly.
1 Baste the cording to the edge of the fabric, but leave about 2 in unbasted at each end. Overlap the ends by about 1 in. Rip out a few stitches on the bias strip to expose the cord.

2 Gently pull the fabric and join the ends, as shown below. Press and trim the seam.

3 Unravel the strands of cord for about $\frac{3}{4}$ in. Cut away 2 strands from one end and one strand from the other to reduce bulk. Twist the remaining strands together and bind them securely with thread. The cord should be slightly loose against the fabric, so that the ends will not pull apart.

4 Fold the bias strip over the cord and finish basting it to the main fabric.

MITERING CORNERS
There are several kinds of miter, suitable for different situations, but the purpose of each is the same: to reduce bulk and to make the corner neat and square.

TO MITER THE CORNER OF A HEM:

1 First mark the fold line for the finished edge. Half-way between this fold line and the edge, mark another fold line. Mark 2 parallel lines diagonally across the corner: one just touching the inner fold line and the other – a cutting line – about $\frac{3}{4}$ in outside the first and parallel to it.

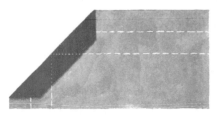

2 Cut off the corner along the cutting line and fold in the fabric on the inner diagonal line; press.

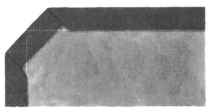

3 Fold in the long edges along the outer fold line; press.

4 Fold again along the inner fold line so that the edges meet at the corner; press. Hem the long edges and join the diagonal edges with overcasting.

This method can also be used to hem one fabric over another – for example, to bring a lining over the edges of a quilt top.

TO MITER BINDING ON A CORNER:

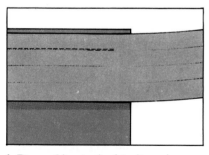

1 Pin and baste the binding along one raw edge, with right sides together and edges matching. Stitch along the crease, ending at the intersection of the seamlines.

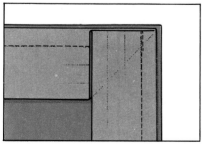

2 Fold the remaining length of binding back over the stitched length as shown, forming a 45° fold across the

corner; press. Pin, baste, and stitch the binding to the fabric edge, taking the stitching all the way to the end.

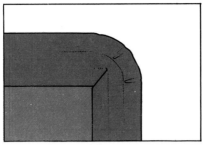

3 Press the binding away from the garment. This reveals the miter formed in the upper edge of the binding.

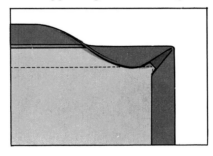

4 Fold the binding to the wrong side; fold it diagonally over the corner, and then turn in the edges as shown. Pin, baste, and slipstitch the edges in place. Slipstitch the folds of the miter together.

GRADING SEAM ALLOWANCES
Where it is important to reduce bulk at a seam, the seam allowances can be trimmed to different widths. This graduated trimming, or "grading," prevents a bulky ridge which could be visible on the right side. Grading is especially important where several layers of fabric – and possibly a layer of batting – are involved.

PRE-SHRINKING FABRIC
To pre-shrink fabric, immerse it, loosely folded, in hot water and leave it for half an hour. Squeeze out the water and hang up the fabric to dry, leaving it folded. Iron the fabric to remove creases.

If you are unsure whether or not a fabric needs to be pre-shrunk, cut a 3 in square of it and draw around the square on a piece of paper. Immerse

the piece in water as described above, then iron it. Compare it with the drawn shape to see whether the fabric will shrink.

To shrink non-woven or iron-on interfacing, hold a steam iron over it for a few moments.

ENLARGING A DESIGN
A number of the designs given in this book must be enlarged before they can be transferred to fabric. The scale of the full-size design is given on the page – for example: "Each square = 2 in." This means that each small square of the printed grid corresponds to a 2 in square on the enlarged design.

To enlarge the design you will need a sheet of graph paper ruled in 1 in squares, a ruler, and a pencil. You may also find it helpful to use a flexible curve, which is a length of plastic that can be used as a guide when drawing curved lines.

If the scale is one square to an inch, you can use the graph paper as it is; however, if it is one square to 2 in, or 3 in, for example, you should first darken every second or third line to create a grid of the correct size. If the scale is a fraction of an inch, you may need to mark off and rule a completely new grid on a blank sheet of paper.

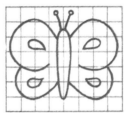

Copy the design freehand from the small grid to the larger one, working on one square at a time. Draw any straight lines first, then fill in curves and details. To draw a curved line that goes across several squares, note carefully at what points the design lines intersect the grid lines, and mark these points at the equivalent places on the large grid. Join up these points with a smooth line. Continue until the whole design has been redrawn to the desired size on the larger grid.

(Some photocopying services will enlarge images mechanically.)

INDEX